Higgidy's founder and chief pie maker, Camilla Stephens, began making pies in 2003, having trained as a cook at Leiths School of Food and Wine. She worked as head of food development for Starbucks UK before leaving to follow her dreams and start her own business – Higgidy. Since then, Higgidy has become one of the UK's fastest-growing food companies making glorious everyday food to help people live well. From wholesome pies and quiches to sausage rolls and mini muffins, its products are now stocked in the UK's major supermarkets.

Camilla is married to Higgidy's co-founder James, and they have two children. *Clever with Veg* is Camilla's third book, and once again her mission is to move more veggies from the edge to the centre of the plate and to empower home cooks to have the confidence to experiment.

T0271632

CLEVER
WITH
VEG

CLEVER
WITH
VEG

Fabulous, fuss-free
vegetarian recipes

Camilla Stephens

MITCHELL BEAZLEY

Contents

GET CLEVER WITH VEG

Life these days can be a bit of a whirlwind. We're all busier than ever before, but many of us still want to eat more conscientiously and let vegetables take centre stage. How do we square these two things? How do we eat the kind of food that's both planet-friendly and life-friendly? The answer is simple: we need to get clever with veg.

For me, this means gloriously easy roasting-tin suppers and faff-free one-pan wonders. It means the judicious use of crafty (yet quality) shop-bought shortcuts. And it means finding ingenious ways to pack more veg into our cooking, as well as strategies for cutting down on food waste.

The recipes in this book reflect how I cook at home, doing everything I can to encourage more of those sitting-down-together moments. The recipes in 'Family Favourites in Under an Hour' include prep and cooking time within the hour, which is pretty good going for a satisfying family meal. Take Scruffy Cauli Cheese Rigatoni (page 14), a particular favourite of my teenage daughter: this recipe cleverly sidesteps the time-consuming béchamel sauce, and instead uses mascarpone to impart a wonderful creaminess.

'Fuss-Free Roasting Tin' focuses on throw-it-together recipes, where everything is cooked in, you guessed it, a single roasting tin. This lets the oven do the lion's share of the work, with very little washing up to do at the end. Even the prep is kept to a minimum thanks to my tips and hacks for using frozen veg, good-quality jars of spice paste and precooked pulses to make things quick and easy. Sesame, Ginger & Broccoli (page 75) is a go-to midweek meal and ready in 30 minutes.

With 'Speedy Salads & Small Plates', my aim is to convince you that even the simplest of dishes can be a thing of joy. I can't stop making Tomato & Cucumber (page 80), with its zingy dressing inspired by the flavours of Thailand. And I hope you'll be tempted by my bread-free Roasted Courgette Bruschetta (page 119) as a summery snack or starter.

In 'Parties & Gatherings', the recipes are longer and require a little forethought. But pop on an apron, along with your favourite podcast, and I hope you'll find cooking for friends and family rewarding and therapeutic. I've included tips to help you get ahead, and I promise that, before you know it, you will have pulled off a masterpiece of veggie gloriousness, such as our Celebration Pie or Soured Cream & Herb Cheesecake (pages 130 and 148). And if you're in the mood for entertaining and need some menu help, head over to page 209 for a host of suggestions to make the process as stress-free as possible.

Finally, I just couldn't write a cookbook without including some puds. At Higgidy, we've become pretty good at baking with veg, and are constantly finding ways to cram an extra portion of sweet potato, butternut squash or carrot into our recipes. So in 'Veg-Packed Puds & Sweet Treats', you'll find a quick brunch recipe for American-style pancakes made with sweet potato mash (page 172); a teatime treat of chocolate chip cookies with curly kale (page 188); and a simple yet very grown-up sorbet made with lemon and cucumber (page 203).

I strongly believe that food can and should be a force for good in the world. Most of us know that the best thing we can do for the planet is to eat less meat and more veg. Well, the recipes here aim to consider both the wider world and our immediate environment too. The resulting dishes are a positive influence on our happiness and the happiness of those closest to us, providing cheerful, thoughtful food that is simple to make and a joy to eat.

My ambition is that this book will prove that creating truly wonderful veggie food doesn't have to be a chore and that you'll feel inspired to cook, serve and eat more veg more often. Most of all, I hope you'll find some recipes you are proud to put on the table at the end of a hard day – and that you'll feel rather jammy knowing it really wasn't hard at all.

USEFUL WAYS TO WASTE LESS

I don't feel good throwing vegetables in the bin. A low-lying guilt creeps over me when I cut into an avocado and instead of bright green flesh it is more of a mushy brown mash. I'm aware that growing food uses vast amounts of the world's natural resources, plus there's the cost of harvesting, transportation and packaging. Added to this when food goes into landfill, the wasted food breaks down to form methane, a greenhouse gas that contributes to climate change. So, here are just a few ideas to help prod and poke you and help you to avoid sweeping those carrot peelings into the bin.

ALL THE TRIMMINGS VEG STOCK

Many of the ingredients that go into making stock are by-products that too often are slung straight in the bin. These include vegetable trimmings, such as the woody ends of asparagus, tough stalks of kale, and limp veg that are looking past their best.

Place the veg trimmings into the stockpot, along with some floppy herbs, unpeeled garlic cloves and even some spices, perhaps a hint of chilli or miso, plus a few peppercorns. Add water, working on the ratio of one to one, so you have the same volume of veggies to water. Cover the stockpot, bring to the boil, then simmer gently for 1 hour. Allow to cool, then strain the stock into a large container, cover with a lid and store in the fridge for up 7 days. Alternatively, decant into a few smaller containers and freeze, ready to be used as you need it.

WASTE-LESS PASTA SAUCE

I have been guilty of scraping the veg trimmings on my chopping board into the bin, but I try not to, and I urge you to try too. Broccoli stalks, cauliflower leaves, kale stems, even peas the children have rejected from supper can be saved for up to four days in the fridge, in a sealable bag or a container with a tight-fitting lid. These oddments can quickly and easily be made into a tasty pasta sauce by combining them with a handful of store-cupboard staples. There's no need to weigh anything, as you can't go wrong.

Start by sautéing a roughly chopped onion or a handful of frozen diced onion in a little oil until just soft. Add 3 or 4 generous handfuls of any veg scraps you have to hand – perhaps limp-looking spinach, floppy courgettes, yellowing broccoli, ageing beans, herb stems or carrot tops, even leftover cooked veg from a Sunday lunch – all chopped to roughly the same size. Pour in just enough water to cover the veg, bring to a simmer and cook, uncovered, for 10 minutes over a medium heat. Set aside to cool, then tip into a blender or food processor, add the juice of half a lemon and 2 or 3 large dollops of cream cheese, crème fraîche or full-fat yogurt, and blitz to a purée. Season generously with salt and freshly ground black pepper, then spoon over freshly cooked pasta, toss well and serve in bowls topped with a grating of Parmesan-style cheese.

BREADY BITS

There are so many ways to give bread a new lease of life that I promise you there's never a reason to throw away even a crust. Here are some of my favourite ways to use up the end of a loaf, a sad-looking bread roll or just odd slices lingering in the bread bin.

PLAIN BREADCRUMBS

If you find you have a sourdough loaf that's past its best, let it go completely stale and then blitz it into crumbs, which I consider a store-cupboard staple. After blitzing, spread them over a tray, and if they still feel a little moist, leave them out to dry. Scoop into a sealable bag and store in the freezer.

FLAVOURED BREADCRUMBS

Once you have blitzed your stale bread as described above, fry the crumbs in a little olive oil, adding a handful of chopped herbs and (if you've got some) a little grated lemon zest. Use to top risottos, salads, stews and pasta dishes, or even to coat some halloumi or paneer cheese.

TOASTS

Cut thick slices of stale sourdough, toast them, then rub them with garlic for bruschetta, which can be topped in any way you like. Alternatively, serve with hummus, a veggie dip or cheese. Another option is to dip the untoasted slices in beaten egg and fry them in a little oil or butter to make French toast (aka eggy bread).

CROUTONS

These are great for sprinkling onto soups, adding to salads or zhooshing up a platter of roasted veggies. Cut or tear stale bread into bite-sized pieces, season with salt and freshly ground black pepper and toss in olive oil. Spread out in a baking sheet and toast in a hot oven (200°C/180°C fan/Gas Mark 6) until golden. Alternatively fry in olive oil and butter over a medium heat until crisp and golden. If you like, add some chilli oil at the end to give the croutons a kick.

LOOK OUT FOR...

Higgidy Hack

→ Throughout the book we've included some Hacks; useful shortcuts to help you to save time or get ahead in your prep.

Higgidy Tip

→ Tips are also included to help you with ideas for new ingredients and substitutions, or ways to get a perfect finish for your dishes.

Family Favourites in Under an Hour

This chapter is about simple, everyday recipes the whole family will love. Tried and tested by the Higgidy team (and, crucially, their nearest and dearest), each one is ready to bring to the table in under an hour. Quick, friendly and fuss-free: this is my kind of cooking.

COURGETTE & CANNELLINI BEAN FRYING-PAN PIE

Vibrant and summery, this simple, satisfying pie is perfect for midweek. Once you've grated the courgettes, the filling takes all of a minute to make, and when that's done, everything happens in the same pan. It's worth spending a little extra on really good fresh pesto, as you really will taste the difference. The same goes for buying good-quality cannellini beans and Italian ricotta.

1. Heat the oven to 190°C/170°C fan/Gas Mark 5.

2. Tip the cannellini beans and their liquid into a bowl. Add the grated courgettes, pesto, lemon zest, chilli flakes and both cheeses. Stir gently until the ingredients are well combined.

3. Brush a 28cm flameproof frying pan with olive oil. Lay a filo sheet in it, letting the pastry overhang the sides, and brush with olive oil. Repeat with a further 4 sheets of pastry, brushing olive oil over each one, and ensuring the whole frying pan is covered by them.

4. Sprinkle the base with the panko breadcrumbs. Spoon the courgette and cannellini bean filling into the pan, on top of the breadcrumbs.

5. Fold the overhanging filo into the centre of the pan. Scrunch any remaining sheets of filo and place them on top to completely cover the filling. Brush with oil.

6. To prevent a soggy bottom, place the pan over a medium heat and cook for 4–5 minutes; you will be able to hear the pastry sizzling.

7. Transfer the pan to the oven and bake for 30 minutes. You can eat the pie immediately, but we recommend letting it cool in the pan for 10–15 minutes so that it sets a little and is easier to cut into generous wedges.

SERVES 6
Ready in 50 minutes

EQUIPMENT
28cm flameproof frying pan

1 × 600g jar large cannellini beans (these are the Rolls-Royce of beans and make all the difference to this dish)

2 courgettes, grated

100g ready-made fresh basil pesto

Zest of 2 unwaxed lemons

Pinch of dried chilli flakes

250g ricotta cheese

50g vegetarian Parmesan-style cheese, grated

Olive oil, for brushing

250g filo pastry (about 6 sheets)

30g panko breadcrumbs

Higgidy Hack

→ This pie can be made and baked a day before serving. The pastry will soften, but you can crisp it up again by loosely covering it with foil and warming in the oven for about 20 minutes.

SCRUFFY CAULI CHEESE RIGATONI

SERVES 4–6 depending on appetites

Ready in 50 minutes

EQUIPMENT

Large flameproof casserole dish with a tight-fitting lid

400g dried rigatoni pasta

3 tablespoons olive oil

1 cauliflower (about 550g), split into small florets

2 leeks, finely chopped

300ml hot vegetable stock

250g mascarpone cheese

250ml single cream

2 teaspoons Dijon mustard

100g smoked Cheddar cheese, finely grated

A handful of chives, roughly chopped

My rustic take on cauliflower cheese sidesteps the classic béchamel sauce, which — let's be honest — can feel like a bit of a faff to make. And the addition of rigatoni transforms it from a tasty side dish into a hearty meal.

1. Heat the oven to 180°C/160°C fan/Gas Mark 4.

2. Bring a large pan of salted water to the boil and cook the pasta according to the packet instructions, until al dente. Drain and set aside in the pan.

3. Meanwhile, place a large flameproof casserole dish over a medium heat, add the olive oil, cauliflower florets and leeks along with 100ml water. Stir well, then cover and cook until soft; this will take about 8 minutes.

4. Add the stock, mascarpone, cream, mustard, half the grated Cheddar and half the chopped chives to the cooked pasta and stir well. (Don't worry if you have a few mascarpone lumps — they will soon melt into the sauce.)

5. Uncover the cauliflower, add the cheesy pasta and stir well to combine into a 'scruffy' mixture. Sprinkle over the remaining smoked Cheddar and bake for 20–25 minutes, or until bubbling and golden. Garnish with the remaining chopped chives just before serving.

Higgidy Hack

→ The whole dish can be prepared in advance and refrigerated for up to 24 hours before baking. In this case, increase the baking time to about 40 minutes to ensure the dish is piping hot right through.

TIKKA MASALA AUBERGINE FLATBREADS

Shop-bought curry pastes save a lot of time that would otherwise be spent chopping and blitzing, and they're an incredible way of packing flavour into veggie dishes. With this recipe, I like to plonk all the elements on the table and let everyone build their own flatbread filling.

1. Preheat the oven to 200°C/180°C fan/Gas Mark 6.

2. Arrange the aubergine pieces in the roasting tin with the paneer. Spoon over the masala paste, drizzle with olive oil and stir to coat evenly. Place on the top shelf of the oven and roast for 35 minutes, turning halfway through. When done, transfer to a serving dish.

3. Meanwhile, place the cherry tomatoes in a small ovenproof dish, drizzle with the olive oil, sprinkle with the brown sugar and stir to combine. Place on the middle shelf of the oven for 25–30 minutes, until the tomatoes are soft, slightly burnished and may well have burst. This is a good sign. Slightly squish the mixture with the back of a fork and tip into a serving bowl.

4. Just before serving, combine the spring onions, coriander leaves and red onion in a small bowl and set on the table, together with the roasted tomatoes, aubergine, paneer and a bowl of yogurt. Warm through the flatbreads and invite everyone to fill their own.

SERVES 4
Ready in 55 minutes

EQUIPMENT
Large roasting tin, about 35 × 25cm; small ovenproof dish

2 large or 3 small aubergines, cut into wedges or thick fingers

250g paneer cheese, cut into 2 × 1cm fingers

4 tablespoons tikka masala paste

3 tablespoons olive oil

FOR THE TOMATOES
400g cherry tomatoes

2 tablespoons olive oil

1 tablespoon brown sugar

FOR THE FRESH ONION SALAD
4–5 spring onions, finely sliced

Handful of coriander leaves, torn

1 small red onion, finely sliced

TO SERVE
Thick Greek yogurt
Flatbreads

SPINACH & COCONUT CURRY
with Oven-Baked Pilaf

SERVES 4

Ready in 50 minutes

EQUIPMENT

Ovenproof dish, about
20 × 30cm

200g baby spinach leaves, washed

400ml full-fat coconut milk

A generous bunch of coriander, stems and leaves roughly chopped

2 tablespoons oil

2 onions, finely diced, or 200g frozen diced onion

2 large garlic cloves, chopped

½ teaspoon ground turmeric

A pinch of dried chilli flakes

150g frozen soya beans

250g cooked Puy lentils

Salt and freshly ground black pepper

FOR THE OVEN-BAKED PILAF

200g basmati rice

400ml boiling water

25g butter, cubed

1 whole red chilli, halved and deseeded

If you've ever suffered the indignity of producing stodgy rice — and who hasn't? — this recipe is a blessing. Baking rice in the oven is way more reliable than cooking it in a saucepan; it gives a wonderful airy texture to the grains, perfect for soaking up the creamy curry mixture.

1. Preheat the oven to 180°C/160°C fan/Gas Mark 4.

2. Start by placing the basmati in a 20 × 30cm ovenproof dish. Pour over the boiling water, add the butter and chilli, and gently combine with a fork. Cover tightly with foil and bake in the oven for 25 minutes. Remove from the oven and set aside to continue cooking in the residual heat of the dish.

3. Place a dry pan over the heat. When hot, add half the spinach and heat for 1–2 minutes, until the leaves have just wilted. Alternatively, cook in the microwave. Transfer to a medium bowl, add the coconut milk and coriander, then blitz with a stick blender until smooth and bright green.

4. Heat the oil in a large saucepan over a medium heat. Add the onions and fry gently, until translucent but without colour. Add the garlic, turmeric and chilli flakes and fry for a further 2 minutes. Tip the remaining spinach into the pan and cook for 1–2 minutes, until wilted.

5. Pour in the green coconut sauce, then add the frozen soya beans and cooked lentils. Stir together and gently simmer for 5–6 minutes. Season with salt and freshly ground black pepper.

6. Uncover the rice and serve in bowls with ladlefuls of the spinach and coconut curry.

Higgidy Tip

→ Packets of cooked Puy lentils are widely available, but if you can't find them or are looking for a substitute, try cooked chickpeas from a jar — they work equally well.

TIKTOK TOMATO PASTA

TIKTOK TOMATO PASTA

SERVES 4 generously

Ready in 40 minutes

EQUIPMENT

Ovenproof dish, about
20 × 30cm

600g cherry tomatoes, or any
good summer tomatoes cut to
an even size

120ml olive oil

200g feta cheese

1 garlic bulb, cut in half
horizontally

400g dried pasta (we like
spaghetti, but you can use
whatever's in your cupboard)

Basil leaves, to serve

**Salt and freshly ground black
pepper**

It was my daughter who alerted me to the TikTok recipe that
went viral and broke the internet – justifiably so in my view.
Easy, quick and unbelievably tasty, this is bung-it-in-the-oven
cooking at its best. Here's our version of it, which I'm sure you'll
agree deserves to be immortalised in print. The tomatoey sauce
can also be served hot with wedges of ciabatta or crusty
sourdough and a summery green salad.

1. Heat the oven to 200°C/180°C fan/Gas Mark 6. Put the tomatoes in a
   20 × 30cm ovenproof dish, pour in half the olive oil and stir to
   combine. Nestle the block of feta and the garlic halves in the centre
   of the tomatoes and pour over the remaining oil. Season well with
   black pepper and bake for 30 minutes.

2. Meanwhile, bring a large saucepan of salted water to the boil and
   cook the pasta according to the packet instructions, until al dente.

3. Remove the tomato dish from the oven and set aside until the garlic
   is cool enough to handle. Peel the garlic cloves, then return them to
   the dish. Using a light touch, mash the garlic and feta with a fork,
   then combine with the roasted tomatoes, without overmixing.

4. Stir the pasta into the tomato mixture, then taste and season if
   needed. Serve in bowls, with fresh basil scattered over the top.

Higgidy Tip

→ If you like your pasta sauce a little thinner, stir a ladleful of pasta
water through the tomatoes and feta once they've been removed
from the oven and mashed together.

← pictured on previous page

OVEN-BAKED RISOTTO THREE WAYS

The traditional method of making risotto involves endless stirring, but my oven-baked version is far more straightforward and every bit as delicious. Choose your topping based on the season, or what you happen to have in your fridge or freezer.

1. Preheat the oven to 200°C/180°C fan/Gas Mark 6.

2. Tip the rice into the large roasting tin. Pour in the vegetable stock and add the butter. Season and stir well. Cover tightly with foil, place in the centre of the oven and cook for 20 minutes. Remove from the oven and stir in the grated cheese, then re-cover and cook for a further 10 minutes. Set aside, still covered, and leave to finish cooking in the residual heat for 5 minutes.

3. While the risotto rice is cooking, prepare your veggies.

→ **Spring** – Cook the peas according to the packet instructions, then add them to the cooked rice along with the pesto. Top with the chopped nuts, pea shoots, if using, and a drizzle of oil.

→ **Summer** – Preheat a grill until very hot. Place the tomatoes and garlic in a roasting tin or grill pan. Drizzle with the chilli oil, and season with salt and chilli flakes. Char under the grill until the tomato skins burst and the garlic begins to crisp. Squish the tomatoes slightly, then spoon on top of the cooked rice and sprinkle generously with freshly shaved cheese.

→ **Autumn** – Spread the butternut squash evenly in a roasting tin. Drizzle with the maple syrup and olive oil, and season with salt and pepper. Roast in the oven while the risotto is baking for 20 minutes, turning once or twice, until lightly caramelised. Stir the squash through the cooked rice and serve sprinkled with toasted pecan nuts and an extra drizzle of oil.

pictured overleaf →

SERVES 4
Ready in 45 minutes

EQUIPMENT
Large roasting tin, about 35 × 25cm, aluminium foil

275g risotto rice

700ml hot vegetable stock

Knob of butter

50g vegetarian Parmesan-style cheese, finely grated

Salt and freshly ground black pepper

SPRING: PEA & PESTO TOPPING

A handful of frozen petit pois

3 tablespoons ready-made fresh basil pesto

40g pine nuts or almonds, toasted and roughly chopped

Pea shoots (optional), for an extra flourish

Olive oil, to drizzle

SUMMER: ARRABBIATA CHERRY TOMATO TOPPING

250g cherry tomatoes

3 garlic cloves, sliced

2 tablespoons chilli oil

Small pinch of dried chilli flakes

Freshly shaved vegetarian Parmesan-style cheese, to serve

AUTUMN: ROASTED MAPLE BUTTERNUT TOPPING

500g butternut squash, peeled and cut into chunks (this can be bought ready-prepared, fresh or frozen)

2 tablespoons maple syrup

1–2 tablespoons olive oil, plus extra to drizzle

Toasted pecan nuts, to serve

ROASTED MAPLE BUTTERNUT

ARRABBIATA CHERRY TOMATO

PEA & PESTO

PLOUGHMAN'S ONE-POT PIE

Pies have a reputation for being tricky to make. Well, that's certainly not the case here. This super-simple, one-pot pie – with its potato, cheese and pickle filling – has an old-fashioned, almost wartime vibe, and is all the more delicious for it. I've made the onion seeds optional because my teens would be put off by them, but I think they give an extra flourish to the pie.

1. Preheat the oven to 200°C/180°C fan/Gas Mark 6.

2. Heat the olive oil in the casserole dish. Add the onions and fry over a medium-high heat until softened and beginning to turn golden brown. Reduce the heat slightly, then stir in the butter and potatoes. Cover and cook over a medium heat for 15 minutes, stirring occasionally, until softened.

3. Pour in the stock and stir well. Add the crème fraîche, chutney and parsley, together with some seasoning. Give it a good mix to combine the ingredients well.

4. Unroll the puff pastry and cut out a disc 2–3cm larger than the pan – you can use the lid of the casserole dish as a guide, and if in doubt, go slightly larger as it will shrink in the oven. Place the pastry gently over the filling (don't worry if it goes up the sides of the casserole a little). Prick with a fork 5 or 6 times, brush with beaten egg and sprinkle over the onion seeds (if using). Bake for 35 minutes, until the pastry is dark golden and the filling is bubbling up around the edges.

SERVES 6 generously

Ready in 1 hour

EQUIPMENT

Large flameproof casserole dish with a tight-fitting lid

2 tablespoons olive oil

2 large onions, roughly chopped, or 300g frozen chopped onion

50g butter

1kg potatoes, peeled and cut into 2cm cubes

200ml hot vegetable stock

300ml crème fraîche

3 tablespoons chutney or pickle

A handful of parsley, roughly chopped

375g ready-rolled puff pastry

Beaten egg, for brushing

2 tablespoons black onion seeds (optional)

Salt and freshly ground black pepper

Higgidy Tip

→ Frozen onions are a staple in my freezer because when I'm in a hurry and cooking a midweek meal, they take 10 minutes off the prepping time and there are no tears. Simply empty them into the pan and treat as you would freshly chopped onion.

CARROT BIRYANI BURGERS

MAKES 6–8

Ready in 1 hour

EQUIPMENT

Large, non-stick frying pan

175g carrots, coarsely grated

250g cooked brown rice

4 tablespoons gram (chickpea) flour

2 teaspoons garam masala

3 garlic cloves, crushed

400g can black beans, drained

1 teaspoon yeast spread (we use Marmite)

2 heaped tablespoons mango chutney

Oil, for frying

Freshly ground black pepper

TO SERVE

Wholemeal pitta breads

Cucumber, cut into thick ribbons or slices

Mint leaves or crunchy lettuce

1 small red onion, finely sliced

Mango chutney

Thick Greek yogurt or tzatziki

Often, when cooking for the family, I'll turn to recipes where the assembly can be done by them at the table. Not only does it save time, but I've found that picky children are far more likely to eat their supper if they think they've made it.

1. Preheat the oven to 180°C/160°C fan/Gas Mark 4.

2. Put the grated carrots, rice, gram flour, garam masala and garlic into the bowl of a blender or food processor. Add the black beans, yeast spread, mango chutney and a generous amount of freshly ground black pepper. Blitz everything into a thick paste.

3. Scrape the paste into a bowl and shape into 6–8 thick patties, about 6cm wide, and dust with a little gram flour. Pop them in the freezer for 10–15 minutes to firm up.

4. Heat a little oil in a shallow, large, non-stick frying pan and fry the burgers over a medium heat for 6 minutes on each side, working in batches if necessary. They should be crisp on the outside. Transfer to a baking sheet and place in the oven for a final 10–12 minutes of cooking.

5. Warm the pitta breads and place them on the table, along with the burgers, the cucumber and other extras. Let everyone fill their own pitta as they like.

Higgidy Hack

→ To get ahead, make the burger mixture 24 hours in advance. Cover and store in the fridge until needed, then shape and cook as above.

VEG BOX HOTPOT

Here's a fab way to use whatever bits and bobs you have left over from your veg box delivery. I usually seem to end up with carrots and potatoes galore, but feel free to swap in whatever roots you have to hand: swede, celeriac and squash all make a brilliant hotpot too.

1. Heat the oven to 200°C/180°C fan/Gas Mark 6.

2. Place the oil in the casserole dish over a medium heat. When hot, add the onion and leek and fry for 5 minutes, until softened.

3. Add the garlic, carrots and thyme and continue to cook, stirring, for a further 5 minutes, until just soft. Stir through the tomato purée, yeast spread, stock and lentils.

4. Crumble the cheese over the lentil mixture, then cover with a layer of potatoes, overlapping the slices. Brush the potatoes with melted butter or, if you're short of time, just dot with knobs of butter.

5. Cover and cook in the centre of the oven for 20 minutes. Remove the lid and cook for a further 20 minutes, until the sauce is bubbling up around the potatoes and the top is golden. We don't think this recipe needs anything else, but if you feel the need for something green, wilt some cavolo nero or spring greens and serve alongside a hearty helping of the hotpot.

SERVES 8

Ready in 1 hour

EQUIPMENT

3-litre shallow flameproof casserole dish with a tight-fitting lid

2 tablespoons olive oil

1 onion, sliced

1 leek, sliced

3 garlic cloves, sliced

3 carrots, peeled and sliced

A handful of thyme leaves, roughly chopped

100g tomato purée

2 teaspoons yeast spread (we use Marmite)

750ml hot vegetable stock

150g split red lentils

75g Wensleydale cheese

3 potatoes (about 300–400g), unpeeled and thinly sliced

Melted butter, for brushing

Higgidy Hack

→ For speed and nutritional value, keep the skin on the carrots and potatoes, and slice using a mandoline.

ALL THE GREENS PAD THAI

These simple noodles are another delicious way to pack more vegetables into your day. In the summer, you should be able to find UK-grown green beans, asparagus, courgettes, pak choi and a ton of other green veg. Whatever you choose, just make sure you've got about 200g of veggies per person.

SERVES 4
Ready in 40 minutes

EQUIPMENT
Large, deep frying pan or wok

200g dried pad thai noodles

2 tablespoons sesame oil

800g fresh green vegetables, such as 2 pak choi, each cut lengthways into 8 pieces; **3–4 spring onions,** roughly chopped; **a handful of asparagus spears,** halved widthways and lengthways; **a generous handful of Tenderstem broccoli; 150g beansprouts**

Zest and juice of 2 unwaxed limes

FOR THE SAUCE

3 tablespoons fish sauce, or vegan 'fish' sauce

1 tablespoon soy sauce

2 tablespoons brown sugar

1 tablespoon tamarind paste

100ml hot vegetable stock

Pinch of dried chilli flakes

TO SERVE

Vegetable oil, for frying

4 eggs

A handful of salted peanuts, roughly chopped

Coriander leaves (optional)

Dried chilli flakes (optional)

1. Mix all the sauce ingredients together in a small bowl. Set aside.

2. Bring a large saucepan of water to the boil. Add the noodles and cook for 2–3 minutes until tender. Drain and cool under cold running water to prevent the noodles sticking together. Set aside.

3. Pour the sesame oil into a large, deep frying pan or wok over a high heat. When hot, add all the vegetables (except the beansprouts) and stir-fry for 3 minutes, until just wilting and catching in the high heat. Toss in the beansprouts, cooked noodles, reserved sauce, lime zest and juice, mix well, then remove from the heat.

4. Heat a little vegetable oil in a frying pan and fry the eggs over a high heat for 2 minutes, until crisp and brown around the edges, but the yolks are still runny.

5. Divide the noodles between 4 shallow bowls, top each with a crispy fried egg, some peanuts, fresh coriander leaves and dried chilli flakes (if using).

NO-FISH FINGERS
with Pea Dip

Crisp fingers of paneer, served hot from the pan, with a cool and creamy green pea dip on the side... delicious! And on the table in just over 30 minutes. If you're really pushed for time, forget the paneer and serve the dip with chopped raw veggies instead.

1. First make the dip. Tip the frozen peas into a bowl, cover with boiling water and leave for 3–4 minutes before draining. Tumble the peas into a blender or food processor, add the cream cheese, half the lemon juice, the garlic, olive oil, mint and some seasoning. Blitz until combined, but still with a slightly coarse texture. Check the seasoning, then spoon into a bowl.

2. Place the flour, eggs and breadcrumbs in 3 separate shallow bowls. Roll the paneer sticks first in the flour, then in the egg and finally in the breadcrumbs.

3. Heat a 1–2cm depth of oil in a large frying pan over a medium-high heat. When hot enough, a cube of bread dropped into it should brown in 20 seconds. Carefully slide the paneer fingers into the hot oil and fry, turning regularly, until golden brown on all sides.

4. Serve the hot paneer fingers with the bright green pea dip.

SERVES 4
Ready in 35 minutes

EQUIPMENT
Large frying pan

50g plain flour

3 eggs, lightly beaten

100g panko breadcrumbs

2 × 200g packets of paneer cheese, cut into long fingers roughly 1.5cm wide

Vegetable oil, for frying

FOR THE DIP

150g frozen peas

150g cream cheese

Juice of 1 lemon

2 garlic cloves, crushed

2 tablespoons olive oil

A large handful of mint leaves, chopped

Salt and freshly ground black pepper

SUMMER MARGHERITA TART

SERVES 6

Ready in 40 minutes

EQUIPMENT

2 baking sheets of about the same size, without rims

A little plain flour, for dusting

A little vegetable oil, for greasing

375g ready-rolled puff pastry

125g cream cheese, softened

2 tablespoons ready-made fresh basil pesto

300g tomatoes, any colour or size (we often use boxes of Isle of Wight tomatoes, which contain a lovely mixture of varieties and sizes), thinly sliced

TO SERVE

Basil leaves

Chilli oil

My Margherita tarts are a riff on the idea of a cheat's pizza: crisp puff pastry with a tomatoey, cheesy topping. This summer version is lighter and brighter, thanks to using fresh tomatoes and aromatic pesto.

1. Preheat the oven to 220°C/200°C fan/Gas Mark 7. Lightly flour one of the baking sheets, and brush the other with oil.

2. Unroll the pastry and place in the centre of the floured baking sheet. Sit the second baking sheet, oiled side down, directly on top of the pastry. This helps to stop the pastry rising too much. Bake for 20–22 minutes, until deep golden brown. Remove the top sheet and allow the pastry to cool.

3. Spread the softened cream cheese over the pastry using a palette knife or the back of a spoon. Spoon over the pesto and arrange the sliced tomatoes on top. Sprinkle with freshly torn basil leaves and a drizzle of chilli oil.

Higgidy Tip

→ Cooking the pastry between 2 baking sheets not only keeps it flat – it produces a beautifully golden base for the tart.

pictured overleaf →

WINTER MARGHERITA TART

Like the previous recipe, this is essentially a cheat's pizza. The puff pastry base in this case is topped with tomato sauce and mozzarella. My children love it, so I sometimes pop wedges into their lunchboxes as an alternative to sandwiches.

1. Preheat the oven to 200°C/180°C fan/Gas Mark 6. Lightly flour one of the baking sheets, and brush the other with oil.

2. Unroll the pastry and place in the centre of the floured baking sheet. Sit the second baking sheet, oiled side down, directly on top of the pastry. This helps to stop it rising too much. Bake for 18 minutes, until beginning to turn golden. Remove the top sheet and allow the pastry to cool for a few minutes.

3. Reduce the oven temperature to 180°C/160°C fan/Gas Mark 4.

4. Mix the pizza sauce and tomato purée together in a bowl, then spread over the pastry using a palette knife or the back of a spoon. Dot the mozzarella over the top, then sprinkle with the grated Cheddar. Bake for 15 minutes, or until the cheese is bubbling.

5. Before serving, cut into 6 squares and top with torn basil leaves.

SERVES 6
Ready in 55 minutes

EQUIPMENT
2 baking sheets of about the same size, without rims

A little plain flour, for dusting

A little vegetable oil, for greasing

375g ready-rolled puff pastry

100g ready-made tomato pizza sauce

50g tomato purée

150–200g mozzarella cheese, torn into pieces

50g mature Cheddar cheese, grated

Basil leaves, to serve

pictured overleaf →

SUMMER MARGHERITA TART

WINTER MARGHERITA TART

SPINACH BUCKWHEAT PANCAKES

Pancakes are a favourite in our home, and the whole batch seems to go very fast. On the rare occasions there are some left over, they can be used with a bit of filling like wraps for a quick lunch the following day.

1. Place the spinach in a blender and add the milk, eggs, flour, salt and paprika. Blitz the mixture at a high speed until it forms a smooth batter. Allow to rest for 10 minutes.

2. Heat a tablespoon of the oil in a 24cm non-stick frying pan over a medium heat. Using dry kitchen paper, wipe the oil around the pan to evenly coat and remove any excess. Once the pan is hot, pour in a ladleful of batter and tilt the pan from side to side to spread it out evenly. Cook on a low–medium heat for 1–2 minutes on each side, until lightly speckled brown. Note: If the heat is too high, the pancake will burn on the outside but not cook through. Keep warm in a low oven until you're ready to serve.

3. Place the pile of pancakes in the centre of the table with a choice of fillings. Dig in immediately.

MAKES 8 depending on size
Ready in 40 minutes

EQUIPMENT
24cm non-stick frying pan

100g young spinach leaves

300ml skimmed milk or oat milk

2 eggs, beaten

150g buckwheat flour

Good pinch of salt

Pinch of paprika

3 tablespoons coconut oil or rapeseed oil

TO SERVE
I try to offer a combo of the following:

→ **A cheese** (e.g. crumbled feta, grated mature Cheddar or a creamy goats' cheese)

→ **A veg** (e.g. some roughly chopped mushrooms sautéed in a little butter, sliced avocado, or sunblush tomatoes)

→ **A soft herb** (e.g. torn basil leaves or roughly chopped dill)

→ **Something moist** (e.g. a smear of thick Greek yogurt, hummus, or fresh pesto)

→ **Some protein** (e.g. fried or scrambled eggs, or scrambled tofu)

VERY QUICK GNOCCHI with Yogurt & Fresh Pesto

SERVES 6
Ready in 30 minutes

EQUIPMENT
Large shallow pan

800g potato gnocchi

30g butter

80g spinach leaves

FOR THE PESTO

30g parsley, leaves and stalks roughly chopped

30g spinach leaves

60g cashew nuts

60g vegetarian Parmesan-style cheese, grated

1 large garlic clove, crushed

Zest and juice of 1 unwaxed lemon

60ml olive oil

Salt and freshly ground black pepper

FOR THE YOGURT BÉCHAMEL

250g thick, full-fat Greek yogurt

100ml cooled vegetable stock

2 egg yolks

1 large garlic clove, crushed

60g vegetarian Parmesan-style cheese, finely grated

Deeply comforting and super-quick, this is just the job for midweek. Here the pesto is made with a mixture of leaves, but you could make it with any soft herb you happen to have, and any type of nut, although cashews do lend a delicious creaminess to a pesto.

1. Start by making the pesto. Put the parsley, spinach leaves, cashew nuts, cheese and garlic into a blender or food processor and blitz to a paste. Add the lemon zest and juice and pulse for a moment to combine. Turning the machine to a slow speed, drizzle in the olive oil and mix until the pesto is smooth and creamy. Season to taste and set aside.

2. Place all the béchamel ingredients in a large bowl. Stir to combine, then set aside.

3. Cook the gnocchi according to the packet instructions.

4. Meanwhile, melt the butter in a large, shallow pan, add the spinach leaves, then cover and cook over a low heat for a minute, or until they have just wilted.

5. Add the gnocchi to the wilted leaves and stir to combine. Pour in the béchamel sauce and heat gently until just warmed through.

6. Spoon the gnocchi into 4 warm bowls and serve with generous dollops of the pesto.

MUSHROOM & CELERIAC STROGANOFF

If you're anything like me, you'll often find half a celeriac languishing at the back of the fridge, waiting for its time to shine. Well, its time has come with this hearty winter warmer, which makes a fabulous veggie alternative to a classic bolognese.

1. Soak the dried mushrooms in the boiling water for 10 minutes.

2. Meanwhile, place the olive oil in the casserole dish over a medium heat. Add the onion and celeriac and cook for 5–7 minutes, or until beginning to soften. Add the fresh mushrooms and cook for a further 5 minutes. Stir through the garlic and the paprika, and cook for 1 minute. Add the soaked mushrooms and their water along with the cider, bring to the boil and reduce the liquid by half. Pour in the veg stock and heat gently, uncovered, for 15–20 minutes.

3. Stir the crème fraîche into the mixture and warm through. Season with salt and a generous amount of black pepper.

4. Heat the butter in a medium saucepan, add the kale and water, and sauté for 3–4 minutes. Meanwhile, cook the pasta according to the packet instructions.

5. Divide the pasta between 4 bowls, ladle the stroganoff mixture over it and top with some buttery kale.

SERVES 4

Ready in 50 minutes

EQUIPMENT

Large flameproof casserole dish; heavy-based frying pan

30g dried mixed mushrooms

150ml boiling water

3 tablespoons olive oil

1 large red onion, finely chopped

½ celeriac (about 250g), peeled and chopped into 1–1.5cm cubes, or roughly grated

250g Portobello or chestnut mushrooms, sliced

3 large garlic cloves, sliced

2 teaspoons smoked paprika

250ml cider

150ml vegetable stock

200ml full-fat crème fraîche

Salt and freshly ground black pepper

TO SERVE

50g butter

80g kale, woody stalks removed

2 tablespoons water

Fresh pappardelle or tagliatelle

LEMONY RAINBOW CHARD & BROAD BEAN BOWLS

If you're pressed for time but find yourself craving something both healthy and satisfying, I have two words for you: bowl food. For me, that usually means stir-fried seasonal veg for flavour, rice or couscous for heft, and a simple sauce to make it all sing. These chard and broad bean bowls are my go-to.

1. Place the olive oil in the casserole dish over a medium heat. Once hot, add the garlic and fry for 1 minute. Add the chilli flakes, courgettes and rainbow chard, turn the heat to high, and fry for 6–7 minutes, until the vegetables soften. Stir in the broad beans and vegetable stock and cook for a few minutes. until the veg are tender. Remove from the heat and stir through the fresh herbs and lemon zest.

2. Meanwhile, place a heavy-based frying pan over a high heat and add the couscous. Toss the grains around the pan for about 4 minutes, until becoming golden. Remove from the heat and immediately add the sultanas and the hot stock. There will be steam and fury. Cover and leave the couscous to soak up the liquid, about 10 minutes. Once the stock has been absorbed, add the lemon juice and stir well. Season with salt and pepper.

3. Divide the couscous between 4 bowls, then top with the rainbow vegetables, a dollop of yogurt and a scattering of lemon zest.

SERVES 4

Ready in 40 minutes

EQUIPMENT

Large flameproof casserole dish; heavy-based frying pan

2 tablespoons olive oil

4 garlic cloves, sliced

½ teaspoon dried chilli flakes

2 courgettes, cut into 2cm cubes

200g rainbow chard, roughly chopped, stalks and all

150g fresh or frozen broad beans, podded

200ml hot vegetable stock

Plenty of herbs (e.g. a mixture of chopped dill and mint)

Zest of 1 unwaxed lemon, plus extra to serve

Salt and freshly ground black pepper

125g thick Greek yogurt, to serve

FOR THE COUSCOUS

200g dried couscous

75g sultanas

250ml hot vegetable stock

Juice of 1 lemon

VEGGIE FALAFEL

SERVES 4

Ready in 1 hour

EQUIPMENT

Large roasting tin, about 35 × 25cm; large, non-stick frying pan

1 butternut squash or 3 sweet potatoes, peeled and cubed (about 450–550g); or a bag of ready-prepared squash

5 garlic cloves, peeled

2 tablespoons olive oil

1 teaspoon dried chilli flakes

2 teaspoons ground coriander

1 teaspoon ground cumin

Pinch of ground turmeric

2 × 400g cans chickpeas, drained

100g dried apricots, chopped into small dice

1 small bunch (about 30g) coriander, chopped

1 small bunch (about 30g) chives, chopped

Juice of 1 lemon

3 tablespoons gram (chickpea) flour or plain flour, plus extra for sprinkling

1 teaspoon nigella or onion seeds

100ml sunflower oil

Salt and freshly ground black pepper

TO SERVE

Pitta breads, hummus, tzatziki, jarred roasted red peppers, lettuce

Good falafel can be very, very good and bad falafel can be horrid! Vacuum-packed ones in particular can be soggy, greasy and high in salt. It's far better to make your own, and this recipe will help you to do that very quickly. If you have any left over, store them in the fridge and add to lunchboxes, or warm through and crumble them over a salad in place of croutons.

1. Preheat the oven to 200°C/180°C fan/Gas Mark 6.

2. Place the squash or sweet potatoes in the roasting tin with the garlic cloves, oil, chilli flakes and ground spices. Season with salt and pepper, then toss everything together to evenly distribute the spices. Place in the oven for 30 minutes, or until just cooked.

3. Place 1 can of drained chickpeas in a blender or food processor. Add the apricots, half the fresh coriander, the warm roasted vegetables and garlic and blitz to a coarse texture. Transfer to a large bowl. Add the second can of drained chickpeas, the remaining coriander, plus the chopped chives, lemon juice and flour. Mix well with your hands to combine.

4. Form the mixture into 16 balls and flatten them gently with the palm of your hand. Sprinkle with the nigella seeds and a little flour.

5. Heat the sunflower oil in a large, non-stick frying pan over a medium heat. Add the falafel in batches and fry gently on each side for 6–7 minutes. Drain on kitchen paper and keep warm in the oven while you cook the remaining batches.

6. Warm the pitta breads in the oven for 5 minutes. Place them on the table, along with the falafel and all the accompaniments, and let everyone dive in.

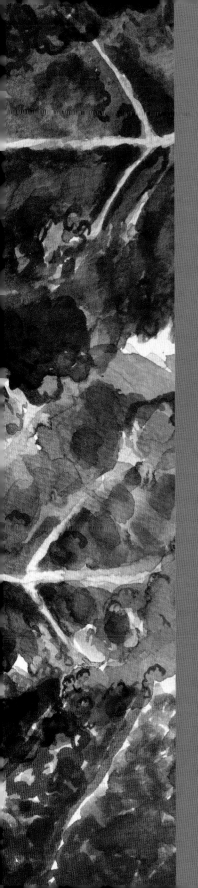

Fuss-Free Roasting Tin

The next few pages are packed
with quick and tasty one-pan
wonders that let your oven
do the hard work for you.
Once you've prepped your
ingredients and popped them
in your roasting tin, it really
is just a case of bung it in and
wait for the magic to happen.

ROASTED ROOT & BLACK BEAN BURRITOS

These hearty, smoky burritos are a doddle to make. Feel free to take a liberty or two with the ingredients — any type of root veg works brilliantly. And if you want to cut down on chopping time, there's no shame in using bags of ready-prepared veg.

1. Preheat the oven to 200°C/180°C fan/Gas Mark 6.

2. Tip the vegetables, onion wedges and garlic into the roasting tin and drizzle over the olive oil. Season well and roast for 25 minutes, stirring halfway through.

3. Remove from the oven and stir in the black beans, chopped tomatoes, chipotle paste, tomato purée and brown sugar. Fill one of the empty 400g cans with boiling water and add to the tin. Mix well and return to the oven to cook for a further 40 minutes, giving everything a good stir at the halfway point.

4. Transfer one-third of the veg mixture to a bowl and blitz to a coarse texture with a stick blender. (This isn't absolutely necessary, but adds variety to the overall texture.) Stir this mixture through the veg still in the roasting tin, then season with salt and pepper to taste.

5. Finally, heat the tortillas according to the packet instructions and serve with the black bean filling, letting everyone build their own burrito using any of the suggested toppings. Eat straight away.

MAKES 12
Ready in 1½ hours

EQUIPMENT
Large roasting tin, about 35 × 25cm

750g root vegetables
(e.g. swede, parsnips, carrots), scrubbed but not peeled, and diced into 1–2cm cubes

2 small red onions, each cut into 2–3cm wedges

2 garlic cloves, halved

3 tablespoons olive oil

400g can black beans, drained and rinsed

400g can chopped tomatoes

2 teaspoons chipotle paste,
or according to taste

2 teaspoons tomato purée

2 teaspoons brown sugar

Salt and freshly ground black pepper

TO SERVE
12 flour or corn tortillas

Toppings: sliced avocado, soured cream, shredded lettuce, lime wedges, grated Cheddar, fresh coriander leaves

Higgidy Hack
→ This recipe makes a generous amount of filling, but leftovers can be frozen for another time, or stored in the fridge for up to 5 days. Reheat thoroughly before serving.

AUBERGINE, TOMATO & HALLOUMI BAKE

SERVES 4

Ready in 1 hour

EQUIPMENT

Large roasting tin, about 35 × 25cm

---

1 preserved lemon

1 red onion, thinly sliced

2 aubergines, cut into fingers 4–5cm long, or chunks

4 tablespoons olive oil

350g cherry tomatoes, some cut in half

250g halloumi cheese, sliced into 8

A small handful of oregano leaves, stalks discarded

70g black olives

Salt and freshly ground black pepper

TO SERVE (OPTIONAL)

Warm couscous

Dukkah (pronounced doo-kah – a traditional Egyptian blend of nuts, seeds and warm spices, now widely available in supermarkets and delis)

Black olives, tender aubergine, squeaky cheese: this is Greece in a roasting tin. Please don't be put off by the preserved lemon – it adds a unique zinginess and can be found in jars at most supermarkets. Failing that, grab a normal lemon, grate a little zest over the tin towards the end of cooking, then squeeze over a smidgeon of juice just before serving.

1. Preheat the oven to 220°C/200°C fan/Gas Mark 7.

2. Cut the preserved lemon in half and use a teaspoon to scoop out and discard the flesh. Shred the rind finely and place in the roasting tin with the red onion, aubergines and half the olive oil. Mix well, season and roast for 20 minutes.

3. Remove the tin from the oven and nestle the tomatoes and halloumi among the aubergine fingers. Drizzle over the remaining olive oil and return to the oven for a further 25 minutes, until the vegetables are soft and the halloumi is beginning to brown.

4. Just before serving, add the oregano and olives to the roasting tin. Place on the table, alongside a bowl of warm couscous, and sprinkle generously with some crunchy dukkah topping if using.

MUSHROOM & KALE OATY CRUMBLE

In this recipe we've used ingredients you might find in a veg box and aren't quite sure what to do with them. Celeriac, for example, is just the root of celery, but somewhat less familiar. Jerusalem artichokes, which are related to sunflowers, have knobbly little roots that have a sweet, nutty flavour when roasted. While both are very tasty, please don't spend hours trying to find them; just swap in parsnips, carrots or whatever else is in the bottom of your fridge.

This dish, so wholesome and comforting, is exactly the kind of food I want to eat on a cold, dark, drizzly evening. There's no need for side dishes here – just place the roasting tin on the table and let everyone dive in.

1. Preheat the oven to 200°C/180°C fan/Gas Mark 6.

2. Place the olive oil in the roasting tin and add the celeriac, artichokes, mushrooms and thyme. Stir to coat, then season well with salt and pepper. Roast for 25 minutes.

3. Meanwhile, make the crumble. Place the oats and butter in a bowl and use your fingertips to rub them together until evenly combined. Add the crumbled cheese, then set aside.

4. Remove the roasting tin from the oven and lower the temperature to 190°C/170°C fan/Gas Mark 5. Stir the kale, cannellini beans and mascarpone through the roasted veg. Add the stock and stir again.

5. Sprinkle the crumble mixture over the veg and return the tin to the oven for a further 30–35 minutes. Allow to cool for a few minutes before serving.

SERVES 6

Ready in 1½ hours

EQUIPMENT

Large roasting tin, about 35 × 25cm

2 tablespoons olive oil

½ celeriac (about 250g), peeled and cut into 2–3cm cubes

150g Jerusalem artichokes, scrubbed and cut into chunks

350g mixed mushrooms, thickly sliced

A handful of thyme leaves, finely chopped

200g curly kale, roughly chopped

400g can cannellini beans, rinsed and drained

250g mascarpone cheese

400ml vegetable stock

Salt and freshly ground black pepper

FOR THE CRUMBLE

200g porridge oats

100g butter, at room temperature

100g crumbly cheese, such as Cheshire or Lincolnshire Poacher

pictured overleaf →

MUSHROOM & KALE OATY CRUMBLE

BUTTERNUT BAKLAVA

SERVES 6 as a main, or 12 as part of a buffet

Ready in 30 minutes, plus cooling time

EQUIPMENT

Large roasting tin, about 35 × 25cm

1 large butternut squash, peeled and diced into 2cm cubes

2 onions, finely chopped, or 200g frozen diced onion

2 teaspoons cumin seeds

400g can chickpeas, drained

3 tablespoons olive oil

2 tablespoons harissa paste

50g dried breadcrumbs

Zest of 1 unwaxed orange

100g butter, melted

2 × 270g packs filo pastry

200g feta cheese, crumbled

½ teaspoon dried chilli flakes

Salt and freshly ground black pepper

Warmed runny honey mixed with chilli flakes, to drizzle

Simple green salad, to serve (optional)

Baklava is typically a dessert of crisp filo pastry with honey and nuts, but here I've layered the filo with sweet, roasted butternut squash and salty feta cheese – and it really does work! Enjoy it warm or cold as part of a vegetarian feast, or pack it for a picnic.

1. Preheat the oven to 200°C/180°C fan/Gas Mark 6.

2. Put the squash, onions, cumin seeds and chickpeas in the roasting tin and drizzle over the olive oil. Add the harissa, season well and toss everything together. Roast for 40 minutes, until the squash is just tender. Set aside to cool for 10 minutes, then use a potato masher to break down any large pieces and leave a rough-textured mixture. Transfer to a bowl and stir in the breadcrumbs and orange zest. Season generously.

3. To make the baklava, wipe out the roasting tin, then brush the base and sides with melted butter. Spread a sheet of filo inside so that it comes slightly up the sides of the tin to create a container. Brush with butter and top with another sheet. Repeat until you have used 4 sheets of filo and have created a container for the filling.

4. Spoon half of the butternut mixture over the filo, sprinkle with half the feta, and cover with 3 further sheets of filo, brushing each with butter as you go. Top with the remaining butternut mixture, sprinkle with the rest of the feta, then add 3 final sheets of filo, again buttering each sheet as you go. Score with the traditional baklava diamond pattern, brush with butter and sprinkle over the chilli flakes. Bake for 35 minutes, or until golden brown. Allow to cool for 30 minutes, then cut into diamonds along the score lines and drizzle with warm honey mixed with a pinch of chilli flakes. Serve with a simple green salad on the side, if liked.

SQUASH & CHICKPEA TAGINE

I like to think of this sweetly spiced tagine as a posh veggie stew. We've used squash, but if you have a sad-looking carrot or two in the bottom of your fridge, throw those in too. It's worth buying a good-quality tagine paste, as it brings a lot of depth to the finished recipe.

1. Preheat the oven to 200°C/180°C fan/Gas Mark 6.

2. Place all the ingredients, from the oil through to the cinnamon stick, in the roasting tin and use your hands to mix everything together. It will look unpromising, but fear not.

3. Cover the tin tightly with foil and roast for 45 minutes. Remove the foil, then roast for a further 45 minutes, or until the veggies are just beginning to catch and the sauce is slightly thicker and sticky.

4. Spoon into bowls and top with the toasted almonds, a dollop of yogurt and a sprinkling of coriander. Serve with the flatbreads.

SERVES 6

Ready in under 2 hours

EQUIPMENT

Large roasting tin, about 35 × 25cm

2 tablespoons olive oil

2 red onions, cut into wedges

750g squash or sweet potatoes, peeled and cut into bite-sized pieces

4 garlic cloves, cut in half

400g can chickpeas, drained

4 tablespoons tagine paste (we like Belazu)

100g pitted Medjool dates, cut in half

400ml hot vegetable stock

400g can chopped tomatoes

1 tablespoon runny honey

Zest of 1 unwaxed lemon, peeled into strips (use a vegetable peeler)

1 cinnamon stick

TO SERVE

A handful of flaked almonds, toasted

Greek yogurt

Coriander leaves, finely chopped

Flatbreads

Higgidy Tip

→ Covering the roasting tin with foil is essential because it mimics an authentic tagine dish, in which steam rises up the lid and condenses before trickling back down into the stew, keeping it moist and saucy.

WINTER VEG YORKSHIRE PUDDING

SERVES 4 generously

Ready in 1 hour 20 minutes

EQUIPMENT

Large roasting tin, about 35 × 25cm

350g carrots, scrubbed and cut into 4–5cm chunks

2 parsnips, scrubbed and cut into 4–5cm chunks

3 banana shallots or 1 large red onion, cut into wedges

3 tablespoons olive oil

Salt and freshly ground black pepper

Buttery winter greens, to serve

FOR THE BATTER

225g plain flour

Pinch of baking powder

4 large eggs

300ml semi-skimmed milk

1 teaspoon Dijon mustard

2 sprigs of rosemary, leaves picked and roughly chopped

FOR THE ONION GRAVY

200g frozen diced onion

Knob of butter

2 tablespoons olive oil

Pinch of dried thyme

1 tablespoon plain flour

400ml vegetable stock, white wine or light ale

1 teaspoon Dijon mustard

Pinch of sugar

Whenever I have a load of winter veg that are about to go past their best, I turn to this recipe. Any roots will work – sweet potato, celeriac, squash... It's a case of using up what you have. The sticky roasted veg are doused in the batter, which rises around them like a squishy pillow.

1. Preheat the oven to 200°C/180°C fan/Gas Mark 6.

2. Put the carrots, parsnips and shallots in the roasting tin and drizzle with the olive oil. Season well and roast for 25 minutes, tossing the vegetables halfway through.

3. Meanwhile, make the batter. Sift the flour and baking powder into a large bowl, then make a well in the centre. Crack in the eggs, then add the milk and mustard. Using a whisk, beat to make a smooth batter. Stir in the chopped rosemary and season well.

4. Working quickly, pour the batter around the roasted vegetables, trying not to coat them completely – it's lovely to see a few bits poking out. Return to the oven for 25 minutes, until the batter is golden and puffed up.

5. While the pudding cooks, make the onion gravy. Place the onion, butter, olive oil and thyme in a saucepan over a very low heat. Cover and cook for 20 minutes. Uncover, add the plain flour and mix well. Stir in the remaining ingredients and simmer, uncovered, for 5 minutes more.

6. Serve the Yorkshire pudding and roasted vegetables in generous portions with buttery winter greens and the onion gravy on the side.

Higgidy Tip
→ This isn't a recipe to scrimp on the oil. Used generously, hot oil will encourage the batter to rise.

COURGETTE & GOATS' CHEESE TORTILLA

Instead of spending an age standing at the stove, turning out individual omelettes for all and sundry, why not let your oven do the work for you? This family-sized baked tortilla is delicious, and if there are leftovers, they're great in packed lunches.

1. Preheat the oven to 200°C/180°C fan/Gas Mark 6.

2. Place the potatoes in the roasting tin, drizzle over the olive oil and season with salt and pepper. Toss gently until the potatoes are evenly coated, then roast for 30 minutes, turning halfway through the cooking time.

3. Meanwhile, break the eggs into a large bowl and whisk for a couple of minutes. Add the courgettes, garlic, chilli, vegetarian Parmesan and half the herbs, and stir together.

4. Remove the tin from the oven and lower the temperature to 180°C/160°C fan/Gas Mark 4. Loosen the potatoes with a spatula, then add a touch more oil to the roasting tin and pour the egg mixture over the hot potatoes. Dot with the goats' cheese rounds and remaining herbs, then return to the oven for 30 minutes, or until firm to the touch. Allow to cool for 20 minutes, then score into 6 squares. Take to the table and allow everyone to help themselves.

SERVES 6
Ready in 1 hour 10 minutes, plus cooling time

EQUIPMENT
Large roasting tin, about 35 × 25cm

750g baby new potatoes, any largeish ones halved or quartered

2 tablespoons olive oil, plus extra for drizzling

10 eggs

2 courgettes, grated

2 garlic cloves, crushed

1 red chilli, deseeded and finely chopped

50g vegetarian Parmesan-style cheese, finely grated

3 tablespoons finely chopped herbs (basil, dill, fennel fronds, chives)

125g goats' cheese log, cut into 5mm rounds

Salt and freshly ground black pepper

Higgidy Tip

→ My mother-in-law hates goats' cheese and reminds me regularly, so if you have a family member who shares the same sentiment, a mixture of feta, ricotta and Cheddar works well.

pictured overleaf →

COURGETTE & GOATS' CHEESE TORTILLA

NEW POTATOES & GREEN BEANS with Rocket Pesto

This simple-to-rustle-up warm salad celebrates some of my favourite ingredients: homemade pesto, British new potatoes (the best, in my view) and creamy burrata. It will more than hold its own as part of a celebration menu, but I usually serve it as a simple, summery supper.

1. Preheat the oven to 190°C/170°C fan/Gas Mark 5.

2. Begin by making the pesto. Place the rocket, garlic, cashew nuts and cheese in a blender or food processor and blitz to a paste. With the machine running at a slow speed, drizzle in the oil, blitzing until the mixture is smooth and creamy. Season to taste and set aside.

3. Place the potatoes in the roasting tin, drizzle with olive oil and roast for 20 minutes. Remove from the oven and coat with half the pesto, then roast for a further 20 minutes.

4. Meanwhile, bring a pan of water to the boil, add the beans and simmer for 3–4 minutes, until just tender. Drain and set aside to keep warm.

5. Tip the beans over the top of the the roasted potatoes, spoon over the remaining pesto and torn burrata. Season with black pepper and serve warm topped with a few extra rocket leaves.

SERVES 4
Ready in 1 hour

EQUIPMENT
Large roasting tin, about 35 × 25cm

750g new potatoes, scrubbed and any large ones quartered or halved (Pink Fir Apples are my favourite, but Jersey Royals work just as well)

Olive oil, for roasting

200g fine green beans, topped and tailed

1 ball of burrata cheese (about 150g)

FOR THE ROCKET PESTO

60g rocket, plus extra to serve

2 garlic cloves

50g cashew nuts

100g vegetarian Parmesan-style cheese, finely grated

130ml olive oil

Salt and freshly ground black pepper

CHEESE & ONION GALETTE

Huge thanks to Nicki in our food team for this one. She and her family tested umpteen different cheese, potato and onion combinations, and came up with what I think is an absolute star of a recipe. Nicki and family, we salute you!

1. Preheat the oven to 220°C/200°C fan/Gas Mark 7. Place a baking sheet on the middle shelf of the oven to heat up. Line a second baking sheet with baking paper.

2. Unroll the pastry and place on the lined baking sheet. Using a fork, prick the pastry all over.

3. Tip the herbs in a bowl, then add the cream cheese and half the grated cheese. Stir well and spread the mixture over the pastry, leaving a 1cm border around the edge.

4. In a bowl, mix together the potato and onion slices, add the olive oil and toss to coat. Arrange them in an even layer over the cheese. Scatter the remaining grated cheese over the veggies and season with black pepper. Brush the border of the pastry with beaten egg.

5. Place the baking sheet with the galette directly on top of the hot baking sheet in the oven. This will help to avoid the pastry developing a soggy bottom. Bake for 20–25 minutes, or until golden brown and the edges have crisped up.

6. Allow the galette to cool for 10 minutes before drizzling with a little runny honey and a scattering of thyme leaves if you wish. Slice and eat with a simple green salad on the side.

SERVES 4–6
Ready in 1 hour

EQUIPMENT
2 baking sheets; large roasting tin, about 35 × 25cm

375g ready-rolled puff pastry

1 small bunch (about 30g) chives, chopped

A handful of basil leaves, torn

100g cream cheese

150g Gruyère cheese or mature Cheddar cheese, grated (Gruyère gives a nutty flavour, but mature Cheddar works equally well)

1 potato (100–120g), unpeeled but very thinly sliced on a mandoline

1 small red onion, very thinly sliced

2 tablespoons olive oil

1 egg, beaten

Freshly ground black pepper

TO SERVE (OPTIONAL)
Runny honey
A small handful of thyme
Green salad

TIKKA ROASTED CAULI CURRY

I love cauliflower and I love curry, so I just had to include this recipe – charred tikka cauli florets in a creamy coconut and spinach sauce. All you need is some fluffy rice on the side and a gloriously puffy garlic naan for dipping. Heaven!

1. Preheat the oven to 200°C/180°C fan/Gas Mark 6.

2. Put the coconut oil, cauliflower, sweet potato, chilli flakes, coriander seeds and tikka paste in the roasting tin, then use a large spoon to toss them around so that everything is well coated in the spices and oil. Roast for 35 minutes, turning once during cooking.

3. Add the coconut milk and spinach to the tin and stir to combine. Return to the oven for 8–10 minutes, or until the spinach has wilted and the coconut sauce is hot. Remove from the oven and stir well. Serve with the rice and warm naan breads.

SERVES 4

Ready in 1 hour

EQUIPMENT

Large roasting tin, about 35 × 25cm

2 tablespoons coconut oil

1 cauliflower, cut into florets

2 sweet potatoes (about 250g), scrubbed and cut into chunks

½ teaspoon dried chilli flakes

1 teaspoon coriander seeds

2–3 tablespoons tikka paste, to taste

400ml can coconut milk

200g baby spinach leaves

TO SERVE

Oven-Baked Pilaf (see page 18)

Warm naan breads

Higgidy Tip

→ It's important to ensure your coconut milk is full fat here, to achieve a creamy sauce.

SPRING VEG PANZANELLA SALAD

SERVES 6

Ready in 35 minutes

EQUIPMENT

Large roasting tin, about 35 × 25cm

200g slightly stale ciabatta or sourdough bread, torn or cut into 2–3cm chunks

4 tablespoons olive oil

150g mixed mangetout and sugar snaps, left whole or cut in half lengthways

1 bunch of asparagus (about 250g), woody ends discarded, then spears cut in half

3–4 spring onions, finely sliced

50g peas, defrosted if frozen

1 small fennel bulb, very thinly shaved on a mandoline

2 Little Gem lettuces, leaves separated

Salt and freshly ground black pepper

FOR THE DRESSING

60ml extra virgin olive oil

2 tablespoons white wine vinegar

1 teaspoon Dijon mustard

1 teaspoon sugar

1 teaspoon capers

Handful of soft summery herbs (e.g. dill, mint, basil, oregano), roughly chopped

pictured overleaf →

Panzanella originated in the Italian countryside, where enterprising home cooks would combine surplus vegetables with slightly stale bread for surprisingly delicious results. The name comes from *pane* (bread) and *zanella* (soup bowl).

1. Preheat the oven to 200°C/180°C fan/Gas Mark 6.

2. Place the bread in the roasting tin and drizzle with half the olive oil. Roast for 15 minutes, or until golden and crunchy. Season and transfer to a plate.

3. Place the mangetout, sugar snaps, asparagus and spring onions in the empty roasting tin (no need to wash it). Drizzle with the remaining olive oil and cook in the oven for 15 minutes.

4. Meanwhile, place the dressing ingredients in a clean screwtop jar and shake well to combine.

5. Place the peas, fennel shavings and lettuce leaves in a large serving bowl. Add the hot veg and crispy croutons, pour over the dressing and toss lightly to combine.

Higgidy Tip

→ To make this dish more substantial, you can add some crumbled feta cheese and a handful of pitted green olives.

WINTER VEG PANZANELLA SALAD

As you might imagine, this is more substantial than the summer version of panzanella. With its hearty roots, roasted grapes (yes, really) and salty blue cheese, it's a great way to use up excess veg.

1. Preheat the oven to 200°C/180°C fan/Gas Mark 6.

2. Place the bread in a large roasting tin with half the olive oil and toss well. Set aside.

3. Pour the remaining olive oil into another roasting tin, add the onion, garlic, sweet potatoes, parsnips and turnip, and toss to coat. Season well and roast for 25 minutes, until the vegetables are beginning to turn golden. Remove from the oven, add the rosemary and chestnuts and stir well.

4. Place the grapes into a small, ovenproof dish and return everything (1 dish and 2 roasting tins) to the oven. Roast for 10–15 minutes.

5. Transfer the roasted vegetables and toasted bread to a large serving bowl, drizzle with the honey and olive oil, and scatter over the blue cheese and parsley.

SERVES 6
Ready in 50 minutes

EQUIPMENT
2 large roasting tins, about 35 × 25cm

200g slightly stale ciabatta or white sourdough bread, torn or cut into 2–3cm chunks

4 tablespoons olive oil

1 small red onion, finely sliced

2 garlic cloves, crushed

2 small sweet potatoes, peeled and cut into 2–3cm chunks

2 parsnips, peeled and cut into 2–3cm chunks

1 small turnip (about 220g), scrubbed and cut into 2–3cm chunks

A large sprig of rosemary, leaves picked and roughly chopped

180g whole cooked chestnuts

200g red grapes

Salt and freshly ground black pepper

TO SERVE

1 tablespoon runny honey

1 tablespoon olive oil

150g blue cheese, crumbled

A handful of flat leaf parsley, roughly chopped

Higgidy Tip

→ Whether to peel a turnip depends on the appearance of the skin: if it looks leathery and tough, peel it; if it's slightly see-through, a light scrub is all that's needed.

pictured overleaf →

SPRING VEG PANZANELLA SALAD

WINTER VEG PANZANELLA SALAD

ROASTED RED PEPPERS
with Spinach & Feta

SERVES 4

Ready in 1 hour

EQUIPMENT

Large roasting tin, about 35 ×
25cm; small frying pan

---

3 Romano red peppers, halved
and deseeded

2 tablespoons olive oil, plus
extra for greasing

1 onion, finely chopped, or 100g
frozen diced onion

2 garlic cloves, finely chopped

250g frozen chopped spinach,
defrosted and excess moisture
squeezed out

4 eggs, beaten

**A small bunch (about 30g) of
herbs** (e.g. mint or dill), finely
chopped

200g feta cheese, crumbled

Freshly grated nutmeg

Freshly ground black pepper

TO SERVE (OPTIONAL)

Warm flatbreads

Olives

Hummus

We have a saying at Higgidy – everything's better with feta. Here
I've combined it with two other Higgidy favourites: red peppers
and spinach. Do try to get hold of Romano peppers if you can.
They look like huge chillies, but are mild and sweet, and work
perfectly in this recipe.

1. Preheat the oven to 190°C/170°C fan/Gas Mark 5. Grease the roasting
   tin with a little olive oil.

2. Arrange the peppers cut-side up in the prepared tin and set aside.

3. Place the olive oil in a small frying pan over a medium heat. When
   hot, add the onion and garlic and fry for 4–5 minutes, until the
   onion is just soft. Transfer to a bowl, add the spinach and eggs, and
   stir well. Add the herbs, 150g of the crumbled feta and a good grating
   of fresh nutmeg and freshly ground black pepper.

4. Spoon this wet mixture into the halved peppers, sprinkle with the
   remaining feta and bake for 35–40 minutes. Serve with warm
   flatbreads, olives and hummus if you wish.

SESAME, GINGER & BROCCOLI

My preferred broccoli for this recipe is Tenderstem, but in the UK it's available only from mid-June to mid-November. Regular broccoli or calabrese can be used instead, though, and are grown throughout the winter months. If using calabrese, I suggest cutting it into smaller florets than ordinary broccoli, and keeping some of the stalk.

1. Preheat the oven to 200°C/180°C fan/Gas Mark 6.

2. Spread the broccoli evenly across the roasting tin, then add the sesame oil, garlic and ginger. Using your hands, toss the veg to coat. Roast for 15 minutes.

3. Meanwhile, combine the sauce ingredients in a small bowl and mix to form a thick paste.

4. When the broccoli has roasted for 15 minutes, add the sauce and toss until everything is evenly coated. Add the peanuts and spring onions and return to the oven for 12–15 minutes, to cook the sauce.

5. Heat the rice noodles according to the packet instructions and divide between 3 or 4 bowls, depending on appetites. Top with the sticky peanut broccoli and serve straight away.

SERVES 3–4
Ready in 30 minutes

EQUIPMENT
Large roasting tin, about 35 × 25cm

500g broccoli, ideally Tenderstem

2 tablespoons sesame oil

3 garlic cloves, finely sliced

2 balls of stem ginger, sliced

100g salted, roasted peanuts, roughly chopped

3 spring onions, finely sliced

Rice vermicelli noodles, to serve (the pre-cooked ones work well)

FOR THE SAUCE

2 tablespoons soy sauce

2 tablespoons peanut butter

2 tablespoons stem ginger syrup from the jar

1 tablespoon sesame seeds

Higgidy Tip

→ To switch up the ingredients, swap the stem ginger for grated fresh ginger, and the ginger syrup for runny honey.

Speedy Salads
& Small Plates

These recipes will have you rustling up winning salads and small plates in no time. We'd recommend letting the season dictate which ones to plump for – that way, your ingredients will be at their peak. Not only will they taste amazing, but they'll be packed with goodness too.

SUMMER TWOSOMES

Twosomes are best friends, a perfect
pair, a dynamic duo – two things that
are simply meant to be together.
These twosome salads focus on two
main ingredients – fruit or veg – that
bring out the best in each other, and
a simple dressing to go with them.

TOMATO & CUCUMBER

SERVES 4

Ready in 20 minutes

1 small cucumber

300g colourful tomatoes, halved or quartered

A mixed handful of coriander, mint and Thai basil, roughly chopped

FOR THE DRESSING

1 tablespoon rice vinegar

1 tablespoon fish sauce, or vegan 'fish' sauce (optional)

Zest and juice of 1 unwaxed lime

2 tablespoons sesame oil

1 teaspoon caster sugar

Salt and freshly ground black pepper

My go-to dressing for tomatoes and cucumber has always been balsamic vinegar and extra virgin olive oil, but this Asian-inspired combo of fresh lime, sesame oil and fish sauce might just pip it to the number one spot. And it works so well with the fresh coriander and Thai basil.

1. Slice the cucumber in half lengthways, then use a teaspoon to scoop out the seeds, leaving 2 long boat shapes. Finely slice each of these into thin crescents.

2. Combine the tomatoes, cucumber and herbs in a large serving bowl. In a separate bowl, whisk together the dressing ingredients and season well.

3. Pour the dressing over the tomato mixture and toss gently to combine. Eat straight away.

ASPARAGUS & PEAS

Verdant, lightly cooked veg; hot, crunchy crumbs; creamy, zesty dressing... for a simple warm salad, this packs in a whole lot of tastes and textures. It makes a superior side dish, or serve it on its own as a light lunch.

1. Place a little oil in a frying pan over a medium-high heat. Cut the asparagus into 2–3 cm pieces, then add to the hot pan and cook for 3–4 minutes, turning once halfway through.

2. Meanwhile, cut the mangetout and sugar snaps in half and blanch them, along with the peas, in a pan of boiling water for 1–2 minutes. Drain and refresh under cold water. Place in a bowl, add the asparagus and a little olive oil and toss together. Transfer to a serving platter.

3. Return the frying pan to the heat and warm a little more olive oil. Add the sourdough crumbs and fry over a medium-high heat for 5–6 minutes, until crisp and golden. Season with salt and freshly ground black pepper.

4. To make the dressing, stir the yogurt and lemon juice together in a small bowl. Pour over the warm veg, then sprinkle the crumbs over the top. Garnish with the lemon zest and a handful of pea shoots, if using, and eat immediately.

SERVES 1
Ready in 30 minutes

EQUIPMENT
Large frying pan

Olive oil, for tossing and frying

150g asparagus, woody ends discarded

250g mixed mangetout, sugar snaps and peas

100–150g sourdough bread, blitzed into crumbs

4 tablespoons Greek yogurt

Zest and juice of 1 unwaxed lemon

A handful of pea shoots (optional)

Salt and freshly ground black pepper

POTATOES & SPRING ONIONS

SERVES 4

Ready in 30 minutes

800g Pink Fir Apple potatoes, scrubbed clean and large ones halved

1 bunch of red spring onions, roughly chopped

2 tablespoons capers, drained

2 tablespoons cornichons, sliced

Salt and freshly ground black pepper

FOR THE DRESSING

A handful of parsley, chives or tarragon, roughly chopped

Juice of 1 lemon

A glug of extra virgin olive oil

100ml soured cream

It's worth getting hold of some nice potatoes for this simple salad. I'm a huge fan of Pink Fir Apples, an old English variety with pinkish skin and waxy flesh. Combine the just-cooked potatoes with red-skinned spring onions, toss in a soured cream dressing and you have a jazzy potato salad with very little effort.

1. Place the potatoes in a large saucepan of cold water and bring to the boil. Cook for about 15 minutes, or until just tender, then drain and transfer to a large bowl.

2. To make the dressing, put half the herbs in a small bowl, add the lemon juice, olive oil and soured cream, and mix well.

3. Pour the dressing over the warm potatoes and toss to coat. Add the spring onions along with half the capers and cornichons. Toss again.

4. Transfer to a serving dish, season with salt and pepper, and sprinkle over the remaining herbs, capers and cornichons.

STRAWBERRIES & ROCKET

SERVES 4

Ready in 10 minutes

200g rocket

400g strawberries, halved through the leafy tops

Freshly ground black pepper

FOR THE DRESSING

3 tablespoons extra virgin olive oil

1 tablespoon balsamic vinegar

1 teaspoon honey

Sweet strawberries and peppery rocket make this a salad of contrasts, and it works beautifully. A sprinkle of salty cheese, such as feta or pecorino, would elevate it even further. Whatever you do, please don't remove the strawberry leaves: they're completely edible and full of fibre and vitamin C.

1. Place the rocket and strawberries in a large bowl and gently toss them together.

2. Whisk the dressing ingredients together in a small bowl, then pour over the rocket and strawberries. Transfer to a serving dish and finish with a good twist of black pepper.

COURGETTES & RADISHES

This is a fun salad, both to put together and to eat, and it makes a surprisingly impressive side dish. If you don't have a griddle pan, you can roast the courgettes and radishes in a hot oven, or – even better – cook them on a barbecue.

1. Place a griddle pan over a high heat. Meanwhile, put the courgettes in a bowl, add a little olive oil and use your hands to toss them gently. When the griddle is good and hot, add the courgettes and cook until tender and lightly charred, about 8–10 minutes. Season well and transfer to a serving dish.

2. Set out 4 skewers or bamboo sticks. Thread 6 whole radishes onto each skewer and griddle for 6–8 minutes, turning the skewers halfway through.

3. Combine the dressing ingredients in a small bowl and whisk together until thick and emulsified.

4. Pour the dressing over the courgettes and radishes, then sprinkle with torn mint leaves to serve.

SERVES 4

Ready in 35 minutes

EQUIPMENT

Griddle pan; skewers or bamboo sticks

200g baby courgettes, sliced lengthways

Olive oil, for tossing and frying

300g radishes, trimmed

Salt and freshly ground black pepper

A few mint leaves, to serve

FOR THE DRESSING

3 tablespoons extra virgin olive oil

1 tablespoon lemon juice

1 teaspoon Dijon mustard

1 garlic clove, crushed

pictured overleaf →

POTATOES & SPRING ONIONS

STRAWBERRIES & ROCKET

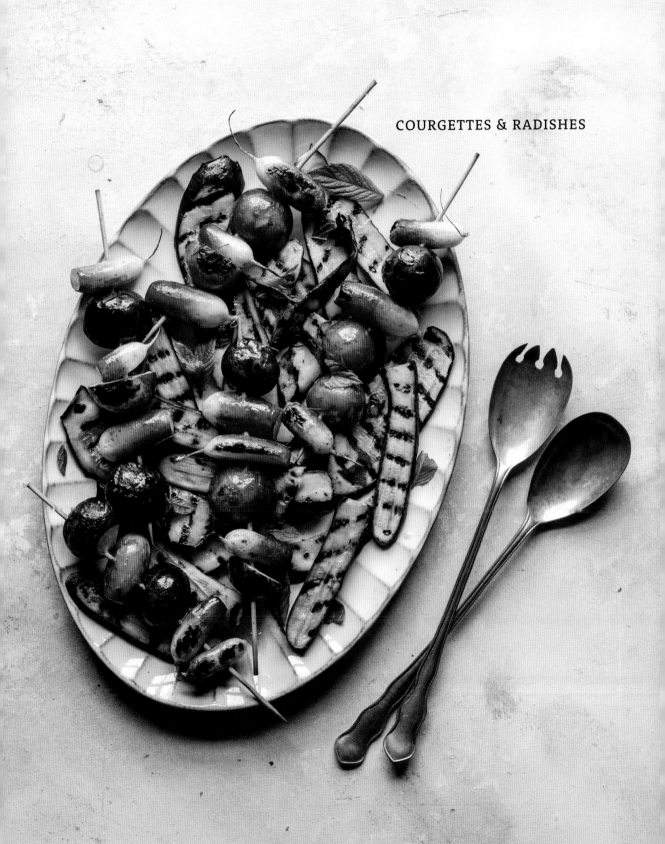

COURGETTES & RADISHES

WINTER THREESOMES

My threesomes bring together three key ingredients to form the basis of a simple winter salad. With each recipe I've included a tip on how to make the dish more substantial, transforming it from a simple side into a hearty main.

PORTOBELLO MUSHROOM, CHICORY & CHESTNUT

SERVES 4

Ready in 35 minutes

EQUIPMENT

Large frying pan

A knob of butter

250g Portobello mushrooms, thickly sliced

2 garlic cloves, peeled and sliced

180g cooked chestnuts, roughly chopped

250g pouch of cooked Puy lentils

A handful of flat leaf parsley, finely chopped

Juice and zest of 1 small orange

3 tablespoons olive oil

A dash of runny honey

Salt and freshly ground black pepper

1 head of red chicory, leaves separated, to serve

Portobello mushrooms are the same variety as white button mushrooms, but browner and much larger versions of their younger selves. If you can't find them, button or chestnut mushrooms work equally well.

1. Melt the butter in a large frying pan over a medium-high heat. Add the mushrooms and fry for 6–8 minutes, stirring occasionally, until softened and lightly golden. Add the garlic and chestnuts and fry for a further 2 minutes. Season well and stir in the Puy lentils.

2. Remove the pan from the heat and stir in the parsley, orange juice, olive oil and honey.

3. Arrange the chicory leaves on a large platter and spoon over the warm mushroom and lentil mixture, and serve with a grating of orange zest.

Higgidy Tip

→ To switch up this dish to a hearty main, massage some kale with olive oil, place in a roasting tin and crisp up in a hot oven (200°C/180°C fan/Gas Mark 6) for 5–8 minutes. Stir into the mushroom mixture with lentils, then arrange on a platter (as above) and crumble over some feta cheese.

pictured overleaf →

WATERCRESS, FIG & WALNUT

Peppery watercress plus sweet, ripe figs and toasted walnuts is a superb combination, and makes a wonderful winter salad. Full disclosure: watercress is a semi-aquatic plant, and in the UK grows best during the warmer months. If you want to stay true to eating seasonally, just swap the watercress for some baby kale during colder periods.

1. Place a small frying pan over a medium heat. Once hot, toast the walnuts for 3–4 minutes, until they are fragrant and just charring. Alternatively, if you have the oven on for something else, spread the nuts in a roasting tin and toast them for a few minutes, until just beginning to brown. Set aside to cool for a minute or so.

2. Place the dressing ingredients in a small bowl and whisk gently until emulsified. Season to taste.

3. Arrange the watercress on a large platter and add the figs. Sprinkle with the walnuts and spoon over the dressing.

SERVES 4
Ready in 15 minutes

EQUIPMENT
Small frying pan or roasting tin

75g walnuts

80g watercress

6–8 fresh figs, quartered or torn into chunks

FOR THE DRESSING

4 tablespoons extra virgin olive oil

1 tablespoon sherry vinegar

½ teaspoon runny honey

Salt and freshly ground black pepper

Higgidy Tip
→ To switch up this dish to a hearty main, spread some labneh (soft Middle Eastern cheese made from strained yogurt) on a platter, arrange the salad ingredients on top and serve with fresh bread; dark rye and walnut loaves make a good pairing.

pictured overleaf →

PORTOBELLO MUSHROOM, CHICORY & CHESTNUT

WATERCRESS, FIG & WALNUT

RED CABBAGE, APPLE & BLACKBERRY

SERVES 4

Ready in 20 minutes

½ **head red cabbage (about 300g),** finely shredded

2 **small Cox's apples,** cored and thinly sliced, preferably on a mandoline

250g **blackberries**

Salt and freshly ground black pepper

FOR THE DRESSING

200ml **buttermilk**

2 **tablespoons mayonnaise**

A dash of runny honey

2 **tablespoons white wine vinegar**

A handful of dill, freshly chopped, plus extra to serve

This is a posh autumn slaw with a simple sweet-sour dressing based on buttermilk. I find the word 'buttermilk' a little bit misleading, as it seems to suggest a high-fat, buttery milk. In reality, it's lower in fat than regular full-fat milk, and has a tangy flavour, a little like yogurt.

1. Combine all the dressing ingredients in a small bowl and mix well.

2. Place the red cabbage, apples and half the blackberries in a large bowl and pour over the dressing. Mix until the cabbage is well dressed. Transfer to a large platter or salad bowl and sprinkle with the remaining blackberries.

3. Season with salt and freshly ground black pepper. Scatter over the remaining dill, and serve.

Higgidy Tip

→ To switch up this dish to a hearty main, scrub 4 sweet potatoes, prick all over and bake for 40–50 minutes in a hot oven (220°C/200°C fan/Gas Mark 7). Allow to cool slightly, then split open the tops and spoon in a generous helping of the slaw. Sprinkle with some toasted pumpkin seeds before serving.

KALE, PUMPKIN & RED ONION

This salad isn't just delicious, it's good-looking too, thanks to a dramatic combination of orange pumpkin, purply-red onion and dark green kale. I could eat it every week during the winter months, especially now I've managed to convince my children of the joys of crispy kale.

1. Preheat the oven to 200°C/180°C fan/Gas Mark 6.

2. Arrange the pumpkin and red onion in a roasting tin, add half the olive oil, toss to coat and season well. Roast for 35–40 minutes, until tender and lightly charred.

3. Put the kale in a large bowl and drizzle with the remaining olive oil. Using your hands, gently toss to combine, then spread evenly in another roasting tin. Place in the oven and roast for 8 minutes, turning halfway through.

4. Meanwhile, combine the dressing ingredients in a small bowl and mix gently.

5. Once the pumpkin and onion are ready, arrange on a serving platter along with the roasted kale. Spoon over the blue cheese dressing and sprinkle with pumpkin seeds. Season with black pepper and serve the salad warm.

SERVES 4–6
Ready in 1 hour

EQUIPMENT
2 large roasting tins, about 35 × 25cm

1 small pumpkin (about 700–800g), peeled, halved, deseeded and sliced into crescents 2cm wide

2 red onions, cut into wedges

4 tablespoons olive oil

125g kale, washed and any tough stalks removed

Salt and freshly ground black pepper

2 tablespoons toasted pumpkin seeds, to serve

FOR THE DRESSING

A handful of crumbled blue cheese

75ml soured cream

2 teaspoons white wine vinegar

1 teaspoon Dijon mustard

Higgidy Tip

→ To switch up this dish to a hearty main, heat 2 tablespoons of olive oil in a saucepan, add 2 crushed garlic cloves and cook very gently for a couple of minutes. Add a posh jar of cannellini beans, along with their liquid, and simmer for about 8 minutes. Now add 2 tablespoons of crème fraîche, season to taste and use a potato masher to squish the beans. Spread this mash over a large platter, arrange the kale, pumpkin and red onion on top, then sprinkle with the pumpkin seeds and drizzle with the blue cheese dressing.

BEETROOT, RADICCHIO & ORANGE

Try to find candy beetroot or golden beets for this salad, and slice them as thinly as possible before combining with the sweet oranges or clementines. These elements, together with the leaves of bitter radicchio, make for a stunning flavour-bomb of a salad.

1. Slice the beetroot as finely as possible, preferably with a mandoline.

2. Cut the oranges into thin slices. Add to the beetroot along with the radicchio leaves. You can, if you like, make an arrangement on the platter, or just toss the ingredients together. Sprinkle the salad with the pistachios.

3. Drizzle the walnut oil and pomegranate molasses over the salad, then season and serve.

SERVES 4
Ready in 20 minutes

EQUIPMENT
Mandoline for slicing

4 candy beetroots, trimmed and peeled

2 oranges or clementines, pith and outer membranes sliced off

1 radicchio head, leaves separated

A handful of shelled pistachios, roughly chopped

2 tablespoons walnut oil

Pomegranate molasses, for drizzling

Salt and freshly ground black pepper

Higgidy Tip

→ To switch up this dish to a hearty main, warm a pouch of cooked lentils or quinoa and spread over the platter before arranging the veg and fruit on top. You can then add a soft, creamy ricotta cheese on one side of the platter, and serve with ciabatta or focaccia bread.

BIG-BOWL SALADS

While the salads in this section take a little longer to prepare, some elements can be made in advance, and the finished dishes will do you proud at any celebration, feast or gathering. It's worth investing in a big, flat plate or wide, shallow bowl to show off your lovely veggies in all their glory.

MINT & LIME SLAW

This crisp, fresh-tasting salad is a zippy alternative to the usual creamy slaw. It's very portable, so is perfect for picnics, but I would pack the peanuts separately and add them just before serving. It's great with vermicelli noodles, too.

1. Start by making the dressing: put all the ingredients for it in a screwtop jar and shake to combine. If you have time, allow the dressing to sit for a few minutes so that the garlic infuses with the lime juice – it will taste all the better.

2. Put all the salad ingredients in a large bowl, reserving a handful of mint and a quarter of the peanuts for decoration. Pour over the dressing and use a 'lifting' motion with a couple of serving spoons to make sure the whole salad is dressed.

3. Serve with the mint and reserved peanuts sprinkled over the top.

SERVES 8
Ready in 20 minutes

½ **head of sweetheart cabbage,** finely shredded

¼ **small head of red cabbage,** finely shredded

60g **mangetout,** sliced on the diagonal

1 **large green chilli,** deseeded and finely chopped

6 **small spring onions,** finely sliced

1 **large bunch of mint (about 60g),** roughly chopped

150g **salted, roasted peanuts,** roughly chopped

FOR THE DRESSING

2 **garlic cloves,** finely chopped

2 **tablespoons fish sauce, or vegan 'fish' sauce**

1 **ball of stem ginger,** finely chopped

1 **tablespoon stem ginger syrup,** from the jar

Zest and juice of 2 unwaxed limes

Higgidy Tip

→ You can use up any leftover cabbage in a quick pickle. Slice up the cabbage and tip into a sterilized heatproof jar. Heat red wine vinegar until boiling and pour over the cabbage. Allow to cool completely. Seal the jar and store in the fridge for up to 1 week.

BUTTERNUT, BARLEY & BASIL

SERVES 6–8

Ready in 45 minutes

___

EQUIPMENT

Large roasting tin, about 35 × 25cm

___

1 butternut squash (about 800g), peeled, deseeded and cut into 2–3cm chunks

A good glug of olive oil

1.2 litres vegetable stock

200g pearl barley

2 tablespoons sherry vinegar

50g vegetarian Parmesan-style cheese, finely grated

Salt and freshly ground black pepper

A good handful of basil leaves, to serve

I see this hearty salad as an easy, super-tasty alternative to the ubiquitous pasta salad. The pieces of sweet, roasted butternut squash work really well with the nutty pearl barley and salty cheese.

1. Preheat the oven to 200°C/180°C fan/Gas Mark 6.

2. Place the butternut squash in a roasting tin, drizzle over the olive oil and season well. Mix until the squash is well coated. Roast for 25–30 minutes, or until golden and tender.

3. Meanwhile, bring the stock to a simmer in a saucepan and add the pearl barley. Return the stock to a rolling boil, then turn the heat right down, cover the pan with a lid and simmer for 20 minutes, or until the barley is just tender. Drain and place in a large bowl.

4. Add the hot squash to the pearl barley, along with the sherry vinegar, cheese and a little extra olive oil. Gently toss together, then transfer to a big serving bowl and garnish with the basil leaves.

Higgidy Tip

→ For a perfect festive salad, crumble some Gorgonzola cheese over the top too.

pictured overleaf →

WINTER KALE CAESAR

Miso paste is a magical Japanese ingredient that brings an addictive umami quality to everything it touches. It works surprisingly well with European flavours, such as Dijon mustard and Parmesan-style cheese. The secret to making this salad beautifully tender is to massage the dressing into the kale leaves, then leave them for an hour. The kale will have softened and almost absorbed the dressing.

1. Place the kale in a large bowl.

2. Place all the dressing ingredients in a separate bowl and mix until thick and creamy. Pour this over the kale leaves and use your hands to massage it in until the kale has softened slightly. Set aside for 1 hour to soften further.

3. To make the croutons, heat the olive oil in a large frying pan over a medium-high heat. When hot, add the bread and fry for 5–6 minutes, turning regularly until beautifully golden and crisp. Sprinkle with salt and transfer to a bowl.

4. Just before serving, transfer the dressed kale onto a serving plate and sprinkle with shavings of cheese, croutons and capers.

SERVES 6
Ready in 1 hour

EQUIPMENT
Large frying pan

1 large bunch of kale (about 150g), thick stalks discarded, and roughly chopped

FOR THE DRESSING
3 tablespoons extra virgin olive oil

Juice of 1 lemon

2 garlic cloves, crushed

1 teaspoon Dijon mustard

1 tablespoon miso paste

2 tablespoons finely grated vegetarian Parmesan-style cheese

FOR THE CROUTONS
4 tablespoons olive oil

½ sourdough loaf (about 200g), torn into pieces

Salt

TO SERVE
Shavings of vegetarian Parmesan-style cheese

1 tablespoon capers, drained

pictured overleaf →

WINTER KALE CAESAR

BUTTERNUT, BARLEY & BASIL

ORZO & SEMI-DRIED TOMATOES

SERVES 6

Ready in 2–3 hours

EQUIPMENT

2 large roasting tins, about
35 × 25cm

750g cherry tomatoes, halved

100ml olive oil, plus extra for
greasing

200g orzo pasta

1 large garlic clove, crushed

2 tablespoons capers, drained

**1 tablespoon white wine
vinegar**

A handful of dill, finely chopped

**Salt and freshly ground black
pepper**

This is a good prepare-ahead salad. I've suggested using cherry tomatoes, but chopped big ones would be delicious too. Either way, cook them slow and low – this will drive off the excess moisture and you'll end up with intense little mouthfuls of sweet tomato nestling within the orzo.

1. Preheat the oven to 160°C/140°C fan/Gas Mark 3. Grease the bases of 2 roasting tins with a little olive oil.

2. Arrange the tomatoes, cut side up, in the prepared tins. Season with salt and pepper, drizzle with half the olive oil and roast for 2–3 hours. When done, any excess liquid should have evaporated away, and the tomatoes should be semi-dried, soft and slightly caramelised. Set aside.

3. Bring a large pan of water to the boil, add the orzo and cook for 3–4 minutes, stirring occasionally, until just soft. Drain and return to the pan with the remaining olive oil and the crushed garlic. Stir to combine.

4. Add the semi-dried tomatoes, capers, vinegar and half the dill. Again, stir to combine.

5. Transfer the salad to a bowl and serve warm, scattered with the remaining dill.

HISPI CABBAGE & BUTTERBEAN MASH

Also known as hearted or sweetheart cabbage, hispi cabbage has a pointy shape and is sweeter than the regular variety. Keep the core in and it will retain its shape brilliantly when cooked, making an elegant centrepiece, especially if topped with emerald green salsa and jewel-like pomegranate seeds.

1. Preheat the oven to 200°C/180°C fan/Gas Mark 6. Place a griddle pan over a high heat until very hot.

2. Brush the hispi wedges with olive oil and place on the hot griddle until golden all over and marked with charred lines. Transfer to a roasting tin, place in the oven for 8–10 minutes until tender, then season.

3. To make the mash, pulse the garlic in a blender, then add the butterbeans and cumin and pulse again. While the motor is running, gradually add the lemon juice and zest through the hole in the lid, followed by the oil. Pulse until the mash is evenly mixed. If it seems very thick, add 2 tablespoons of the reserved butterbean liquor. Taste and adjust the seasoning if necessary.

4. To make the salsa, pulse the garlic and herbs in a small blender. Add the chilli and continue to blend while slowly adding the oil and finishing with the vinegar.

5. To assemble the salad, spread the mash over a warm platter and top with the griddled cabbage wedges. Spoon over the vibrant herb salsa and decorate with the pomegranate seeds. Serve immediately.

SERVES 4–6, depending on cabbage size

Ready in 45 minutes

EQUIPMENT
Griddle pan; large roasting tin, about 35 × 25cm

1 large hispi cabbage, trimmed and cut into 6 wedges

Olive oil, for brushing

Salt and freshly ground black pepper

Seeds from 1 pomegranate, to serve

FOR THE MASH
2 garlic cloves

700g jar posh butterbeans, drained, but liquor reserved

Large pinch of ground cumin

Zest and juice of 1 unwaxed lemon

50–80ml olive oil

FOR THE SALSA
2 garlic cloves

1 small bunch (about 30g) coriander, stalks and leaves

1 small bunch (about 30g) mint, stalks discarded

1 red chilli, deseeded and finely chopped

120ml olive oil

1 tablespoon vinegar

ALLOTMENT FATTOUSH

SERVES 6

Ready in 45 minutes

EQUIPMENT

Large roasting tin, about 35 × 25cm; baking sheet

400g can chickpeas, drained

Olive oil, for drizzling

1 tablespoon sumac

2 pitta breads, cut into 2–3cm squares

300g colourful summer tomatoes, halved

½ cucumber, diced

200g radishes, either the little red spheres, or the elongated French Breakfast variety, sliced

A large handful of mint and parsley, roughly chopped

Salt and freshly ground black pepper

Basil leaves, to serve (optional)

FOR THE DRESSING

2 tablespoons extra virgin olive oil

Juice of 1 large lemon

Fattoush is essentially a Mediterranean fried bread salad. We've added toasted, spiced chickpeas to bring some heft, and the result is a hearty, wholesome salad packed full of flavour and very easy to throw together. A crowd pleaser, indeed.

1. Preheat the oven to 200°C/180°C fan/Gas Mark 6.

2. Tip the chickpeas into a roasting tin and drizzle with a little olive oil. Sprinkle over the sumac and a good pinch of salt. Mix well and roast for 20–25 minutes, until golden, tossing halfway through. Allow to cool for a few minutes.

3. Drizzle the pitta squares with a little olive oil and season with salt and pepper. Spread them out on a baking sheet, place in the oven and bake for 10 minutes.

4. Arrange the tomatoes, cucumber and radishes all in a large bowl with the herbs, cooled chickpeas and toasted pitta squares. Dress with the olive oil and lemon juice. Serve with a handful of basil leaves, if liked.

NECTARINE, CUCUMBER & SOFT SUMMER HERBS

This recipe is so easy, but really only works if you make it at the height of summer. The nectarines must be ripe, and the cucumber a wonky one grown here in Britain. Mixed with soft herbs, topped with creamy burrata, and served with some holey ciabatta on the side to mop up the dressing, it's a joy.

1. Slice the nectarines into 1cm slices and arrange on a platter. Add the cucumber slices, torn burrata, herbs and a twist of salt and pepper.

2. Drizzle the salad with olive oil and serve.

SERVES 6
Ready in 10 minutes

3 nectarines, halved and stones removed

1 cucumber, finely sliced

1 ball of burrata cheese (about 150g), torn into pieces

2 handfuls of soft herbs (e.g. basil, mint, flat leaf parsley, dill, chives)

2 tablespoons extra virgin olive oil, for drizzling

Salt and freshly ground black pepper

SMALL PLATES & DIPS

Every now and then I just want to do the 'chip and dip' thing. I'll open a bag of fancy tortilla chips, smash an avocado into some hummus, and then whip up a few veggie crudités to create a colourful board. Here are a few of my favourite recipes to turn a simple spread into a veggie feast.

MISO AUBERGINE

Salty, savoury miso paste gives a lovely depth of flavour to all kinds of dishes, and is particularly delicious when combined with honey, ginger and sesame seeds. I think you'll find these velvety aubergines difficult to resist. I suggest serving them with pre-dinner drinks, or alongside a stir-fry or noodle dish.

1. Preheat the oven to 220°C/200°C fan/Gas Mark 7. Lightly oil a large roasting tin.

2. Score the cut sides of the aubergine halves with a knife, making shallow cuts in a criss-cross pattern and being careful not to cut through the skin. Place in the prepared tin.

3. Combine the paste ingredients in a small bowl and mix well. Spoon this paste on top of the aubergine halves, trying to get as much as possible into the cuts. Sprinkle each half with sesame seeds, then roast for 30–35 minutes, until the aubergines have slightly collapsed and charred. The edges will be sticky and caramelised.

4. Serve hot, garnished with coriander leaves.

SERVES 4
Ready in 45 minutes

EQUIPMENT
Large roasting tin, about 35 × 25cm

Oil, for greasing

2 large aubergines, cut in half lengthways

2 tablespoons sesame seeds

Coriander leaves, to garnish

FOR THE PASTE

2 tablespoons white miso paste

2 tablespoons runny honey

3 tablespoons vegetable oil

2 tablespoons sesame oil

2 garlic cloves, crushed

1 thumb of fresh root ginger, peeled and grated

HONEY-ROASTED BLACKENED BRUSSELS SPROUTS

SERVES 6 as a pre-dinner nibble

Ready in 1 hour

EQUIPMENT

Large roasting tin, about 35 × 25cm

750g Brussels sprouts, trimmed

Olive oil

4 tablespoons runny honey

2 garlic cloves, crushed

Salt and freshly ground black pepper

In my view, Brussels sprouts are unfairly maligned. Some people complain that they have a strong, sulphurous flavour, but that's only if you boil the life out of them. To avoid any risk of that, just roast them instead, and they take on a charred, crispy moreishness that's hard not to love. In fact, there's a pub at the foot of the South Downs that serves crispy sprouts as an appetiser. Good for them!

1. Preheat the oven to 220°C/200°C fan/Gas Mark 7.

2. Place the sprouts in a roasting tin. Drizzle with olive oil and roast for 30 minutes, turning halfway through. Reduce the oven temperature to 200°C/180°C fan/Gas Mark 6.

3. Warm the honey, a dash of olive oil and the garlic in a small saucepan for a couple of minutes before pouring over the sprouts. Mix well to combine, season with salt and pepper and transfer to the top shelf of the oven for a further 20 minutes, turning halfway through, until the sprouts have blackened and become sticky. Serve piled into a bowl with plenty of seasoning.

ROASTED GARLIC HUMMUS

SERVES 6
Ready in 45 minutes

EQUIPMENT
Roasting tin

---

1 garlic bulb, cut in half horizontally

3 tablespoons olive oil, plus extra for drizzling

¼ teaspoon ground cumin

¼ teaspoon ground coriander

400g can chickpeas, drained

2 tablespoons tahini

Juice of ½ lemon

Salt and freshly ground black pepper

Pitta breads, to serve

Shop-bought hummus is tasty and very convenient, but if you're in the mood for something special, this homemade version – with its sticky roasted garlic – is just divine. Serve with batons of crisp, raw veg or some warmed-through pittas.

1. Preheat the oven to 200°C/180°C fan/Gas Mark 6.

2. Place the garlic in the centre of a roasting tin, drizzle with olive oil and sprinkle over the cumin and coriander. Roast for 25–30 minutes, until the garlic is soft. Allow to cool slightly before squeezing the garlic flesh into the bowl of a blender or food processor.

3. Add the chickpeas, tahini, olive oil, lemon juice and seasoning, and blitz until just smooth. Taste and add a touch more salt or lemon juice if you think it's needed.

4. Spoon into a bowl, drizzle with extra olive oil and serve with a pile of warm pitta breads.

pictured overleaf →

ROASTED COURGETTE BRUSCHETTA

This is ideal for anyone wishing to cut down on carbs. Instead of piling the topping onto toasted bread, as is traditional with bruschetta, we're using roasted courgettes as our base. Choose chubby courgettes, as you can fit more of the herby cream cheese on top, and take care not to overcook them.

1. Preheat the oven to 220°C/200°C fan/Gas Mark 7.

2. Slice the courgettes in half lengthways, then widthways, so you have 12 pieces in total. Place them in a roasting tin, drizzle with olive oil and season well. Roast for 20 minutes, then turn the oven down to 200°C/180°C fan/Gas Mark 6 and roast for a further 20 minutes, until the courgettes are lightly firm and golden.

3. Meanwhile, combine the cream cheese, herbs, lemon zest and juice in a small bowl and mix well.

4. Once the courgettes are cooked, set aside to cool before topping each piece with a spoonful of the cream cheese mixture.

5. Just before serving, sprinkle the pine nuts, parsley and lemon zest over the topped courgettes.

SERVES 6
Ready in 1 hour

EQUIPMENT
Large roasting tin, about 35 × 25cm

3 courgettes, ends trimmed

Olive oil, for drizzling

Salt and freshly ground black pepper

FOR THE TOPPING
100g cream cheese

A handful of mixed fresh summer herbs (e.g. basil, parsley and mint), chopped

Zest and juice of 1 unwaxed lemon

TO SERVE
A handful of toasted pine nuts

Chopped parsley

Zest of 1 lemon

pictured overleaf →

ROASTED GARLIC HUMMUS

CAULIFLOWER 'POPCORN'

SERVES 6 as a side
Ready in 45 minutes

EQUIPMENT
Large, heavy-based saucepan

500ml vegetable oil, for frying

1 large cauliflower, broken into bite-sized florets

FOR THE BATTER

250g plain flour

2 garlic cloves, crushed

2 teaspoons smoked paprika

2 teaspoons ground turmeric

A good pinch of salt

2 tablespoons chopped coriander leaves, plus extra to serve

300ml cold sparkling water

Salt

In my experience, children love cauliflower and they love popcorn. As a result, these bite-sized deep-fried morsels of cauliflower, which look a lot like popcorn, go down a treat — and not just with kids. They're best eaten immediately, although it's unlikely anyone will hold back.

1. Begin by making the batter. Place all the ingredients for it in a bowl, slowly adding the sparkling water and stirring until it forms a smooth, thick batter.

2. Place the oil in a large, heavy-based saucepan over a medium-high heat. When hot enough, a pea-sized amount of battered cauliflower should sizzle immediately. At this point, dip the cauliflower florets into the batter and carefully lower them into the hot oil. Cook in batches if necessary so you don't overcrowd the pan, for 2–3 minutes each batch. Flip regularly to ensure even cooking, until beautifully golden brown all over.

3. Transfer the cooked cauliflower to a large plate lined with kitchen paper to absorb any excess oil. Once it's all cooked, sprinkle with chopped coriander and salt. Eat while still warm.

CORN ON THE COB RIBS

This is finger food at its best: little strips of corn coated in smoky spices and roasted in the oven. They're super-quick to make and really fun to eat. Just be careful when cutting the corn into ribs – it's not difficult, but it does require a sharp knife and a steady hand.

1. Preheat the oven to 220°C/200°C fan/Gas Mark 7.

2. Using a large cook's knife, trim the cobs so the ends are flat, then cut in half lengthways. Stand each half vertically and use a rocking motion to cut right through it from top to bottom. Now cut each quarter in half widthways to create a total of 8 short 'ribs'. Repeat with the remaining cobs.

3. Place the olive oil, paprika, harissa and garlic in a small bowl and stir to combine. Brush the ribs with this mixture, transfer them to a roasting tin and roast for 25 minutes, turning halfway through, until lightly charred.

4. Sprinkle with the chopped coriander and serve with the soured cream on the side.

SERVES 6
Ready in 40 minutes

EQUIPMENT
Large roasting tin, about 35 × 25cm

3 sweetcorn cobs

2–3 tablespoons olive oil

1 teaspoon smoked paprika

1 tablespoon rose harissa

2 garlic cloves, crushed

TO SERVE
Handful of coriander, roughly chopped

Soured cream

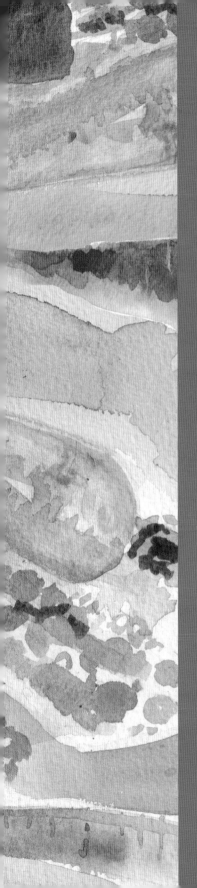

Parties & Gatherings

Cooking for a crowd can be daunting. But with the right recipes, it absolutely doesn't have to be. In this section, I have included both main courses (showstopping dishes that are surprisingly easy), and starters and snacks to hand around while the main event it in the oven.

ASPARAGUS & CHIVE TART

SERVES 4–6

Ready in 1 hour, plus chilling

EQUIPMENT

Baking sheet

2 eggs

160g cream cheese

40g vegetarian Parmesan-style cheese, finely grated

20 fine asparagus spears, trimmed and woody ends discarded

A handful of chives

Salt and freshly ground black pepper

Chive flowers, to garnish (optional)

FOR THE YOGURT PASTRY

200g plain flour, plus extra for dusting

100g cold butter, cubed

45g Greek yogurt

2 tablespoons cold water (optional)

A quick and very easy pastry made with flour, butter and yogurt, topped very simply and brimming with summeriness. If you have any chive flowers, they can really jazz it up.

1. Start by making the pastry. Place the flour and butter in a bowl and rub together with your fingertips until the mixture resembles breadcrumbs. Add the yogurt and stir until a dough starts to form. If it's looking a little dry, add a tablespoon or two of cold water to help bring the pastry together in a ball. Place it on a lightly floured surface and knead gently for a minute, or until smooth. Wrap the dough in cling film and chill in the fridge for 20 minutes.

2. Preheat the oven to 200°C/180°C fan/Gas Mark 6. Line a baking sheet with non-stick baking paper.

3. Roll the pastry into a rectangle on a lightly floured surface until it's roughly 20 × 30cm. Transfer to the prepared baking sheet.

4. Beat 1 egg in a bowl. Add both cheeses, season with salt and pepper and beat until well mixed. Spread evenly over the pastry, leaving a 2cm border all round the edges. Arrange the asparagus and chives on top.

5. Beat the remaining egg in a small bowl and brush it around the pastry border. Bake for 25–30 minutes, or until the pastry is golden and the asparagus is beginning to char. Cool for 15 minutes, then garnish with chive flowers (if using) and serve.

CELEBRATION PIE

SERVES 10–12

Ready in 3¼ hours, plus chilling

EQUIPMENT

3 roasting tins; 24cm springform cake tin

450g sweet potatoes (about 3), peeled, halved and sliced

3 large courgettes, cut into 5mm thick slices

3 red peppers, deseeded and cut into quarters

2 tablespoons olive oil

Butter, for greasing

3 tablespoons dried breadcrumbs

3 cooked beetroot (about 250g), sliced

A handful of basil leaves, torn

4 large eggs plus 2 egg yolks

250ml double cream

50g vegetarian Parmesan-style cheese, freshly grated, plus extra for topping

Salt and freshly ground black pepper

FOR THE HOT-WATER CRUST

125g salted butter, diced

1 teaspoon salt

180ml water

375g plain flour, plus extra for dusting

There is always something impressive about bringing a pie to the table – it is a work of art that demonstrates real care and thought. I make no apology for the fact that this special pie requires some time to put together as it's definitely worth the effort. The pastry is a hot-water crust pastry, which forms a robust container for this bounty of summer vegetables. Do take time to roast the veggies well; this drives off excess moisture and ensures the pie will not result in sloppy slices.

1. Preheat the oven to 190°C/170°C fan/Gas Mark 5. Set out 3 large roasting tins.

2. Brush all the vegetable slices with olive oil, season with salt and pepper, then spread them out in the roasting tins, one type of veg per tin. Put the courgette tin on the bottom shelf of the oven, peppers in the middle and sweet potato at the top. Roast for 40 minutes, swapping the pepper and sweet potato tins around halfway through to ensure all the vegetables are tender.

3. Grease the springform tin with butter and line the bottom with a circle of baking paper.

4. To make the hot-water crust, place the butter, salt and water in a medium saucepan over high heat and bring to the boil. Remove from the heat and stir in the flour until a smooth dough forms. Turn onto a lightly floured surface and knead the dough for 2–3 minutes, until smooth.

5. Roll out the dough between 2 sheets of non-stick baking paper to a thickness of 3–4mm. Use the pastry to line the tin, pressing it up the sides and letting it overhang the rim. Trim with scissors to form a neat edge, then chill for 20 minutes.

6. Line the chilled pastry case with a sheet of crumpled baking paper, then fill with baking beans or dried pulses. Bake for 20 minutes, then remove the beans and paper and bake for a further 15 minutes, or until the pastry is golden. Set aside to cool slightly. Reduce the oven temperature to 180°C/160°C fan/Gas Mark 4.

7. Sprinkle the breadcrumbs in the bottom of the pastry case. Top with a layer of roasted sweet potatoes, then beetroot, torn basil, courgette and finally red pepper.

8. Place the eggs, cream and cheese in a bowl and whisk together. Pour this mixture slowly over the veg, easing it gently to allow it to seep into the gaps. Be careful not to let it spill over the edge. Sprinkle with a touch more cheese, then season and bake for 1 hour, or until set and golden. Ideally, allow the pie to rest for at least 1 hour so that the layers firm up, as this makes slicing an easier task. Top with finely grated Parmesan-style cheese to serve.

 Higgidy Hack
→ To get ahead, you can bake the pie the day before it's needed. Cool and store in the fridge, but remove 30 minutes before serving.

pictured overleaf →

CELEBRATION PIE

SUMMER ROLLS

I'm often looking for portable food and these wraps have
become my go-to. They are versatile and lighter than traditional
tortilla wraps. Here are a few of my favourite combinations for
filling them. The ingredients are simply suggestions rather than
precise amounts.

FOR THE WRAPPERS
Fill a large bowl with hot water and open a packet of spring roll rice
paper wrappers. Dip 1 wrapper at a time in the water, leaving it for
about 5 seconds, until soft and pliable. Place the wrapper on a board
and fill with some of the suggestions below.

FOR A MINT, RED PEPPER & AVOCADO FILLING
Cook some rice vermicelli noodles according to the packet
instructions, then drain well. Transfer to a bowl, roughly chop the
noodles and mix with plenty of freshly chopped mint, lime zest and
juice, and a dash of vegan 'fish' sauce. Spoon some of this filling onto
the wrap and top with thin strips of red pepper and sliced avocado.
Roll up and serve with a ready-made peanut dip or some sweet chilli
dipping sauce.

FOR A SWEET POTATO, FALAFEL & SPINACH FILLING
Bake a couple of sweet potatoes. Allow to cool slightly, then scoop out
the flesh and season with salt and freshly ground black pepper. Spread
the sweet potato mash over a softened wrapper (see above) and top
with crumbled falafel (ready-made or see page 44) and fresh spinach
leaves. Roll up and serve with a tzatziki dip.

FOR A PESTO, MOZZARELLA & ROCKET FILLING
Combine some cooked quinoa with fresh pesto, to taste. Sprinkle this
over a softened wrapper (see above) and top with torn mozzarella,
some sweet sundried tomatoes and a handful of peppery rocket
leaves. Roll up and serve with any remaining fresh pesto sauce.

PEA, LEMON & PINE NUT MILLEFEUILLE

SERVES 4

Ready in 50 minutes, plus cooling

EQUIPMENT

2 baking sheets

350g ready-rolled puff pastry

Plain flour, for dusting

150g fresh peas

3 courgettes, sliced into courgetti (use a julienne peeler, spiraliser or box grater)

2 tablespoons olive oil

Zest and juice of 1 unwaxed lemon

250g mascarpone cheese

40g vegetarian Parmesan-style cheese, freshly grated

1 heaped tablespoon toasted pine nuts

Salt and freshly ground black pepper

A millefeuille, or 'thousand sheets', is a sweet dessert, but here it's been given the savoury treatment, with layers of creamy mascarpone, garden peas and courgetti. It's simple, fresh and easy to assemble.

1. Preheat the oven to 200°C/180°C fan/Gas Mark 6.

2. Unroll the pastry and slice into 4 equal rectangles. Transfer 2 to a floured baking sheet and prick with a fork, then repeat with the remaining 2 on a second floured baking sheet. Bake for about 20 minutes, until deep golden brown. Remove from the oven and allow to cool completely.

3. While the pastry is in the oven, place the peas in a small pan of boiling water and simmer for 1 minute. Drain and refresh under cold water to prevent further cooking. Set aside.

4. Place the courgetti in a bowl with the olive oil and half the lemon juice and zest. Season and set aside to macerate for 5–6 minutes.

5. Place the mascarpone in a bowl with the Parmesan-style cheese and remaining lemon juice, season well and mix together.

6. To assemble the millefeuille, secure a piece of puff pastry to a plate with a small blob of the mascarpone mixture. Spread with a quarter of the mascarpone mix, then sprinkle with a quarter of the courgetti and a quarter of the peas. Top with another piece of puff pastry and repeat the layering twice more, finishing with courgetti and peas on top of the final layer of pastry. Sprinkle over the pine nuts and remaining lemon zest. If you can, allow the millefeuille to sit for 10 minutes or so before serving.

RAINBOW FRITTERS

MAKES 12

Ready in 30 minutes

EQUIPMENT

Large frying pan

150g rainbow chard, finely chopped

1 small red onion, finely chopped

1 sweet potato (about 180g), peeled and grated

100ml vegetable oil

Salt

4 tablespoons Greek yogurt, to serve

FOR THE BATTER

3 eggs

80g plain flour

A pinch of celery salt, or salt if preferred

These fritters are aptly named because they contain a colourful assortment of vegetables. They take just minutes to assemble, minutes to cook and minutes to eat!

1. Start by making the batter. Beat the eggs in a large bowl, then beat in the flour and salt.

2. Add the prepared veggies and mix well until thoroughly coated in the batter. To test if the mixture is thick enough, take a large spoonful of it and form into a patty. If it just holds together, it's fine; if not, add a little more flour to the mixture.

3. Place the oil in a large frying pan over a medium-high heat. To check it is hot enough, drop a small blob of batter into the oil – it should sizzle straight away. Use tongs to add small amounts of the batter mixture to it, flattening them slightly with a spatula. Fry for 2–3 minutes, until golden brown on both sides. Transfer to a plate lined with kitchen paper to absorb any excess oil.

4. Sprinkle the fritters with salt and serve with a bowl of Greek yogurt.

pictured overleaf →

HALLOUMI CIGARS with Apricot Jam

Salty halloumi wrapped in crisp filo pastry and served with sweet apricot jam is a delight. These 'cigars' are best eaten on a balmy summer's evening with a glass of rosé.

1. Preheat the oven to 180°C/160°C fan/Gas Mark 4. Line a baking sheet with non-stick baking paper.

2. Cut each filo pastry sheet into 8 equal rectangles and set aside under damp kitchen paper.

3. Brush 1 pastry rectangle at a time with olive oil, add a couple of spinach leaves, then sit a second layer of pastry on top. Place a finger of halloumi along the narrow edge of the pastry and roll into a cigar shape, tucking in the sides as you go. Repeat until you have made 16 cigars in all.

4. Place the cigars on the prepared baking sheet, brush with olive oil and bake for 15–18 minutes, until the pastry is crisp and golden.

5. Place the apricot jam into a bowl and serve alongside the warm halloumi cigars.

MAKES 16
Ready in 40 minutes

EQUIPMENT
Baking sheet

4 sheets of filo pastry

Olive oil, for brushing

A handful of young spinach leaves

250g halloumi cheese, cut into 16 equal fingers

100g apricot jam (I like Bonne Maman apricot compote)

pictured overleaf →

HALLOUMI CIGARS WITH APRICOT JAM

PREPARE-AHEAD QUESADILLAS

RAINBOW FRITTERS

PREPARE-AHEAD QUESADILLAS

Quesadillas are surprisingly adaptable and quick to fling together. Find good-quality, ready-made corn tortillas and pack them with protein, vegetables, grains or whatever else you have to hand, but be sure to include a cheese that can melt, and take care not to overfill them. Here's the pick of our favourite fillings.

FOR A GREENS & BRIE FILLING
Heat a spoonful of oil in a shallow frying pan, add a handful of diced onion, some chopped spring greens, diced green chilli and a handful of frozen peas. Sauté over a low heat until everything is soft and the greens have wilted.

Place a corn tortilla on a dry, flat surface and spread the warm veg mixture over it. Tear or cut some Brie cheese into small pieces and dot them across the filling. Cover with a second tortilla and slide the whole thing into a hot, dry frying pan. Cook over a high heat, turning once, until the cheese has melted and the tortilla is slightly charred on both sides. Slide onto a board and cut into wedges.

FOR A SPINACH, ARTICHOKE & MOZZARELLA FILLING
Defrost a handful of frozen spinach or wilt a small bag of fresh spinach. Place in a bowl and add some cream cheese, a sprinkling of grated mozzarella and some torn artichoke hearts. Mix into a lumpy spread, then season with salt and freshly ground black pepper.

Place a corn tortilla on a dry, flat surface and spread the creamy spinach filling over it. Sprinkle with more grated mozzarella, cover with a second tortilla and slide the whole thing into a hot, dry frying pan. Cook over a high heat, turning once, until the cheese has melted and the tortilla is slightly charred on both sides. Slide onto a board and cut into wedges.

FOR A KALE, APPLE & CHEDDAR FILLING
Heat a spoonful of oil in a shallow frying pan, add a couple of handfuls of kale and a tablespoon of water. Cook over a medium heat until the kale has just softened. Remove from the heat and grate an apple (with skin on) into the kale. Stir well and season with salt and freshly ground black pepper.

Place a corn tortilla on a dry, flat surface, spread the kale and apple filling over it and sprinkle with a generous amount of grated mature Cheddar cheese. Cover with a second tortilla and slide the whole thing into a hot, dry frying pan. Cook over a high heat, turning once, until the cheese has melted and the tortilla is slightly charred on both sides. Slide onto a board and cut into wedges.

GARDEN GREEN LASAGNE

Here's a summer version of a classic lasagne without the hassle. There's no need to make a white sauce or even fry an onion. The main body of work is layering roasted courgettes, fresh spinach, mint and fresh lasagne sheets. Assemble in the morning and bake just before your guests arrive.

1. Preheat the oven to 200°C/180°C fan/Gas Mark 6.

2. Top and tail the courgettes, then cut into diagonal slices 5mm thick. Brush with oil, season and spread out in 2 large roasting tins. Roast at the top of the oven for 45–50 minutes, swapping the tins around halfway through, until tender and beginning to brown.

3. Wilt the spinach by plunging it into a large pan of simmering water for about 1 minute. Drain the spinach into a sieve and squeeze out any excess water.

4. Soak the lasagne sheets in a single layer in boiling water for 5 minutes. (Although the instructions that come with fresh lasagne often say the sheets can be used straight from the packet, I find soaking them improves the texture.) Drain well.

5. Place the crème fraîche in a medium bowl and stir in the cheese. Add a splash of milk to loosen the mixture, and season to taste with salt and pepper.

6. Oil a 2-litre ovenproof dish and line the bottom with a quarter of the lasagne sheets. Cover with a third of the courgette slices, then top with a third of the wilted spinach and mint. Spoon over a quarter of the cheese sauce. Repeat these layers in the same order, until you have used up all the vegetables. Finish with a layer of lasagne sheets then top with cheese sauce and a little extra cheese. Bake for 35–40 minutes, or until the lasagne is golden brown and bubbling.

SERVES 6

Ready in 2 hours

EQUIPMENT

2 large roasting tins; 2-litre ovenproof dish

5 courgettes

olive oil, for brushing

300g baby spinach leaves

1 small bunch (about 30g) mint, stalks removed and leaves finely chopped

250g fresh lasagne sheets

Salt and freshly ground black pepper

FOR THE SAUCE

600g crème fraîche

100g vegetarian Parmesan-style cheese, finely grated, plus extra to serve

A splash milk, to loosen

pictured overleaf →

GARDEN GREEN LASAGNE

MISO AUBERGINE TARTE TATIN

The idea of an upside-down tart that combines miso and aubergine might at first glance seem a little intimidating, but it's actually quite straightforward. Hidden under the buttery puff pastry, the filling appears to collapse into the sticky caramel... until the big reveal. I think there's something romantic about this dish.

1. Preheat the oven to 210°C/190°C fan/Gas Mark 7.

2. Arrange the aubergine slices in a roasting tin, brush with the oil and season well. Roast for 30–35 minutes, turning over halfway through, until they are soft and slightly golden. Set aside to cool slightly.

3. To make the caramel, place the oil and butter in a 28cm ovenproof frying pan over a medium heat, swirling them around until combined. Allow to bubble for about a minute, then take off the heat and add the miso paste, honey and vinegar. Swirl around to combine evenly, then arrange the aubergine slices on top of the miso mixture, adding a second layer if necessary to fit them all in the pan. Set aside.

4. Lightly flour a work surface and roll out the pastry until it is about 4mm thick and large enough to cover the frying pan easily. Using the rolling pin to help lift it, carefully drape the pastry over the pan so that it overhangs the rim evenly. Using scissors, trim the overhang to about 1cm all round. Lightly press the pastry onto the aubergines, then make a few slits in the surface for steam to escape. Bake for 30 minutes, until the pastry is risen and golden brown. Set aside to cool for 10 minutes.

5. Place a lipped serving plate upside-down over the pastry, then, using oven gloves, hold the plate firmly and flip the whole thing over. Remove the pan, replacing any escaped slices of aubergine, and serve immediately.

SERVES 6
Ready in 1½ hours, plus cooling

EQUIPMENT
Large roasting tin, about 35 × 25cm; 28cm ovenproof frying pan

3 aubergines, thinly sliced

2 tablespoons vegetable or sesame oil, for brushing

Flour, for dusting

500g block of ready-made puff pastry

Salt and freshly ground black pepper

FOR THE CARAMEL
2 tablespoons vegetable oil

30g butter

2 tablespoons miso paste

3 tablespoons runny honey

2 tablespoons white wine vinegar

SOURED CREAM & HERB CHEESECAKE

SERVES 8

Ready in 2 hours, plus chilling overnight

EQUIPMENT

20cm springform or loose-based cake tin

Butter, for greasing

400g full-fat cream cheese

200g soured cream

75g Pecorino cheese, freshly grated

2 eggs, lightly beaten

1 garlic clove, crushed

Micro herbs, pea shoots or baby salad leaves, to serve

FOR THE BASE

225g oatcakes

50g walnuts

120g butter, melted

Cheesecake but not as you know it – an oaty biscuit base topped with a soured cream and cheese filling. You'll need to start this the day before serving but it gives a wow factor to any summer celebration. I tend to make this in the summer and top it with micro herbs and baby salad leaves, but you could easily make it in the winter months and top with an array of roasted beetroot and fresh thyme leaves.

1. Preheat the oven to 170°C/150°C fan/Gas Mark 3. Line the base of the cake tin with non-stick baking paper and grease the sides liberally with butter.

2. To make the base, place the oatcakes and walnuts in a blender or food processor and blitz to a fine crumb. With the motor running, pour in the melted butter until the crumbs are coated. Press them firmly into the base of the cake tin using the back of a spoon, then chill in the fridge for 10 minutes.

3. Place the cream cheese, soured cream, Pecorino, eggs and garlic in a bowl and beat with a handheld electric mixer until just combined. Pour the mixture over the oatcake base and bake for 1 hour and 20 minutes, until the sides have set but there is a slight wobble in the centre. Allow to cool, then chill in the fridge overnight.

4. On the day of the party, 30 minutes before serving, carefully remove the cheesecake from the tin and transfer to a serving plate. Top with an array of micro herbs or baby salad leaves.

MUSHROOM STEAKS with Kale & Butterbean Mash

Portobello mushrooms are a great veggie alternative to steak because they are so meaty in texture. Here they are served with a rich and savoury sauce. Pile both on top of the creamy mash for a Friday night treat.

1. Preheat the oven to 190°C/170°C fan/Gas Mark 5.

2. Place the garlic and red onion in a large roasting tin, add the chilli flakes, fennel seeds, tomato purée and olive oil and stir well. Make sure all the ingredients are evenly spread across the tin.

3. Sit the mushrooms, domed-side up, on top of the veggies, pushing them down a little. Cover with a large piece of baking paper, tucking it down around the edges to make sure all the ingredients are enclosed. Place a large sheet of foil over the tin, scrunching it under the rim so that no steam can escape. Cook in the centre of the oven for 30 minutes.

4. Remove the foil and baking paper, turn the mushrooms over and shake the cherry tomatoes around to stop them sticking. Cover with just the foil and return to the oven for a further 20 minutes.

5. Meanwhile, make the mash. Warm the olive oil in a saucepan over a medium heat, then add the garlic, kale and water. Cover and cook gently for about 8 minutes. Lightly squash the drained butterbeans with a fork or potato masher, then stir into the kale along with the cream. Taste and add the lemon zest and juice a little at a time until you get the flavour you want. (Depending on the size of your lemon, you might need only half the zest and juice.) Cook over a low heat for a few minutes, stirring constantly, just to warm the mash.

6. Transfer the mushrooms to a plate or dish and cover with foil and a tea towel to keep warm. Increase the oven temperature to 200°C/180°C fan/Gas Mark 6.

7. Squish a few of the tomatoes and garlic with the back of a wooden spoon to make a rough sauce, then return (uncovered) to the oven for a further 8–10 minutes to reduce.

8. To serve, divide the mash between 4 warm plates, top each with a mushroom and spoon over the tomatoes and juices from the tin.

SERVES 4
Ready in 1¼ hours

EQUIPMENT
Large roasting tin, about 35 × 25cm

6 garlic cloves, peeled

2 red onions, cut into wedges

Generous pinch of red chilli flakes (use more if you like a good amount of heat)

Pinch of fennel seeds

4 heaped tablespoons sundried tomato purée

2 tablespoons olive oil

500g Portobello mushrooms

400g cherry tomatoes

FOR THE MASH

3 tablespoons olive oil

2 garlic cloves, crushed

125g kale

2 tablespoons water

500g canned butterbeans (drained weight)

150ml single cream

Zest and juice of 1 unwaxed lemon

HASSELBACK ROASTED SQUASH

SERVES 6

Ready in 1½ hours

EQUIPMENT

Large roasting tin, about 35 × 25cm

---

1 large squash (e.g. acorn, butternut or kabocha)

1–2 tablespoons olive oil

150ml vegetable stock

50ml apple cider vinegar

Salt and freshly ground black pepper

FOR THE SALSA VERDE

20g basil leaves

30g flat leaf parsley

2 garlic cloves

40g small capers, drained, rinsed and roughly chopped

2 teaspoons Dijon mustard

75ml extra virgin olive oil

TO SERVE

30g tahini

100g Greek yogurt

Here the squash is incised with slashes (hasselbacked) so that the skin becomes crisp and the flesh better absorbs the flavours of the stock and vinegar in which it is roasted. Sitting on top of tahini-flavoured yogurt and eaten with lashings of salsa verde, this is perfect for a winter celebration.

1. Preheat the oven to 200°C/180°C fan/Gas Mark 6.

2. Cut the squash in half lengthways and scoop out the seeds with a spoon. Turn the halves cut-side down and use a sharp knife to make parallel incisions into the skin and flesh every 3–5mm, being careful not to cut all the way through – you want the squash to stay intact (see tip below). If your knife skills allow, experiment with making the cuts in a pattern as shown in the picture.

3. Rub or brush the olive oil over the squash and season with plenty of salt and black pepper. Place cut-side down in a roasting tin, pour the stock and cider vinegar around it and roast for 1 hour, until tender and the skin is beginning to brown.

4. Meanwhile, make the salsa verde. Finely chop the basil, parsley, garlic and capers together on a board. Place them in a bowl, then stir in the mustard, olive oil and some seasoning.

5. Just before serving, combine the tahini and yogurt in a bowl, then spread over a platter. Top with the squash halves and spoon over the salsa verde.

Higgidy Tip

→ Place a wooden chopstick either side of the squash halves while making the parallel cuts to avoid accidentally slicing all the way through the skin.

ROASTED BEETROOT & FETA TART

I never thought I would fall in love with beetroot, but these roasted beets are so far removed from the acidic beets you find in jars, they're a complete revelation. Try to find small fresh beetroot with leafy tufts; once roasted, they and the salty feta are very happy bedfellows.

1. Begin by making the pastry, either by hand (as below) or in a food processor. Sift the flour and salt into a large bowl, add the butter and rub it in with your fingertips until the mixture resembles breadcrumbs. Add the Cheddar and stir to combine. Mix in the beaten egg and a few splashes of ice-cold water, just enough to bring the pastry together. Turn onto a lightly floured work surface and knead lightly and briefly until smooth. (Overhandling the dough will warm the fat and the pastry will turn out tough and chewy.)

2. Preheat the oven to 200°C/180°C fan/Gas Mark 6 and put a baking sheet in the oven to heat up.

3. Lightly flour a work surface and roll out the pastry to about 3mm thick. Lift the pastry by rolling it around a rolling pin and then unrolling it over the 30 × 20cm fluted tart tin. Don't worry if your pastry cracks, just use your fingers to patch the pieces together. Ease the pastry around the tin and then use a rolling pin to roll firmly across the top of the tin to trim away any excess pastry. Prick the base all over with a fork and chill in the fridge for 30 minutes.

4. Meanwhile, put the beetroot in a roasting tin, season well with salt and pepper and drizzle with olive oil. Roast for 30 minutes, or until just soft. Set aside and reduce the oven temperature to 180°C/160°C fan/Gas Mark 4.

5. Remove the tart case from the fridge and line with non-stick baking paper. Fill with baking beans or dried pulses to prevent the sides collapsing and bake on the hot baking sheet for 20 minutes. Remove the beans and paper, then return the pastry case to the oven for a further 10 minutes. This will allow the base to dry out before it is filled.

6. To make the filling, place the eggs, cream and Parmesan-style cheese in a bowl and beat together until just combined. Season well, then pour into the pastry case. Arrange the beetroot inside and sprinkle with the feta and oregano. Bake on the hot baking sheet for 30 minutes, or until the filling is just set and the top is turning golden. Serve with freshly ground black pepper.

SERVES 6–8
Ready in 1¾ hours

EQUIPMENT
30 × 20cm loose-based, fluted tart tin; baking sheet; large roasting tin, about 35 × 25cm

6 small beetroot (about 500g), halved or quartered

Olive oil, for drizzling

3 eggs

300ml double cream

50g vegetarian Parmesan-style cheese, finely grated

200g feta cheese, crumbled

1 small bunch (about 30g) oregano, leaves roughly chopped

Salt and freshly ground black pepper

FOR THE CHEESE PASTRY
200g plain flour, plus extra for dusting

Generous pinch of salt

75g cold butter, diced

50g mature Cheddar cheese, finely grated

1 egg, beaten

BUTTERNUT SQUASH DAMPER BREAD

MAKES a 20cm loaf

Ready in 1¾ hours, plus cooling

EQUIPMENT

Baking sheet; large roasting tin, about 35 × 25cm

1 butternut squash, peeled, deseeded and cut into 2cm cubes (about 300g peeled weight)

2 tablespoons harissa paste

A glug of olive oil

250g self-raising flour, plus extra for dusting

2 teaspoons baking powder

2 tablespoons caster sugar

100g butter, melted

75ml milk

200g feta cheese, crumbled

Salt and freshly ground black pepper

Australian damper bread, traditionally cooked on the coals of a campfire, doesn't involve yeast, so it's quick to make and (in my experience) the whole loaf is eaten in one sitting. I think a homemade loaf stuffed full of cheese and veggies makes for a perfect Boxing Day centrepiece.

1. Preheat the oven to 200°C/180°C fan/Gas Mark 6.

2. Place the squash in a large roasting tin, spoon over the harissa, drizzle with olive oil and season with salt and pepper. Give everything a good stir, then roast for 25–30 minutes, until golden and tender. Remove from the oven and allow to cool for 5 minutes. Reduce the oven temperature to 190°C/170°C fan/Gas Mark 5.

3. While the squash is cooling, sift the flour and baking powder into a large bowl and stir in the caster sugar and a pinch of salt. Make a well in the centre and pour in the butter and milk, stirring as you go. If necessary, add a touch more milk to bring the mixture together; it should form a soft dough. Add the roasted squash and feta. Lightly flour your hands and carefully combine the veggies, cheese and dough, trying not to overhandle the dough, or it will become tough.

4. Turn onto a floured surface and shape into a 20cm round loaf. Using the floured handle of a wooden spoon, press a cross into the surface of it. Place on a baking sheet, cover with foil and bake for 20 minutes.

5. Whip off the foil and bake for a further 25 minutes, or until the loaf sounds hollow when tapped on the bottom. If it isn't ready after this time, turn it upside down and bake for a few minutes more.

6. Transfer to a wire rack, cover with a clean tea towel (this keeps the crust nice and soft) and leave to cool. To serve, break into quarters, then cut each quarter in half to make 8 wedges, or simply slice the loaf. Eat on the same day.

pictured overleaf →

SEEDED BUTTERMILK CRACKERS

I am addicted to these. I make them with a pick and mix of different seeds, whatever I have in my store cupboard. Feel free to experiment and find your winning combination. Serve them with dips, cheeses, soups or as an excellent present; crack into shards, pop in cellophane bags and tie with a bow.

1. Preheat the oven to 180°C/160°C fan/Gas Mark 6 and grease a large baking sheet with oil.

2. Place the flour in a bowl, make a well in the centre, then add the salt and pour in the buttermilk. Using a large spoon, mix together until a dough forms.

3. Flour a work surface and knead the dough on it for 3–4 minutes, until smooth and soft. Using a rolling pin, roll the dough into a very thin rectangle, roughly 30 × 35cm.

4. Ease the rolling pin under the dough to help lift it up, then carefully drape it onto the prepared baking sheet. Prick all over with a fork. Using the back of a spoon, spread the sweet chilli sauce over the dough, being careful not to tear it. Sprinkle over the seeds and use the back of an oiled spoon to gently press them into the dough.

5. Bake for 20 minutes, then use a large spatula or a palette knife to release the cracker from the baking sheet. Reduce the oven temperature to 160°C/140°C fan/Gas Mark 4 and bake the cracker for a further 20 minutes to dry out. Transfer to a wire rack to cool, then snap into shards to serve.

MAKES a 30 × 35cm cracker

Ready in 1 hour

EQUIPMENT

Large baking sheet

Oil, for greasing

150g plain flour, plus extra for dusting

½ teaspoon fine salt

100ml buttermilk

2 tablespoons sweet chilli sauce

60g seeds, such as sesame seeds, caraway seeds, fennel seeds, nigella seeds, poppy seeds, golden linseeds, pumpkin seeds (either a mixture or all one type, whatever you fancy!)

pictured overleaf →

BUTTERNUT SQUASH DAMPER BREAD

SEEDED BUTTERMILK CRACKERS

CHEESE & POTATO BOREKS

CHEESE & POTATO BOREKS

MAKES 16
Ready in 1½ hours, plus cooling

EQUIPMENT
Baking sheet

Flour, for dusting

5 sheets of filo pastry, each about 35 × 30cm

50g butter, melted

FOR THE FILLING

500g King Edward potatoes, peeled and cut into 3–4cm cubes, or 500g frozen mashed potato

2 eggs, lightly beaten

125g Cheddar cheese, coarsely grated

50g mozzarella cheese, coarsely grated

½ teaspoon dried chilli flakes (optional)

Boreks are savoury pastries that originated in the Middle East during the 13th century. Commonly filled with potato, often married with other ingredients, they come in many different shapes and sizes. I've stuck to the popular cheese and potato combination, and layered it between wafer thin filo. Try making these little pies at Christmas instead of sausage rolls.

1. Start by making the filling. Cook the potatoes in a pan of simmering salted water for 10 minutes or so, until just tender. Drain and allow to steam-dry for a minute or so, then mash until smooth. Alternatively, defrost the frozen mash according to the packet instructions. Add the beaten eggs, cheeses and chilli flakes and mix until fully combined.

2. Place a sheet of filo pastry onto a clean work surface. Spread a quarter of the potato mixture over the filo, spreading right to the edges, being careful not to tear the dough. Cover with another sheet of pastry and repeat the spreading. Repeat twice more, until you've used all the potato mixture. Cover with a final layer of filo.

3. Using gentle hands, roll the layered pastry into a cylinder shape. Transfer to a baking sheet lined with non-stick baking paper and place in the freezer for 10–20 minutes, to firm up.

4. Meanwhile, preheat the oven to 180°C/160°C fan/Gas Mark 4.

5. Cut the filo log into 16 equal rounds, about 2cm wide. Return to the lined baking sheet and brush the slices with the melted butter. Bake in the oven for 35–40 minutes, or until golden brown.

← pictured on previous page

CHRISTMAS LEEK, MUSHROOM & CHESTNUT PITHIVIER

A magnificent puff pastry pie stuffed full of veggies and Christmas flavours. You can assemble the whole pithivier the day before and store it in the fridge until you're ready to bake it, but be sure to get the oven really hot so the pastry cooks through.

1. Preheat the oven to 200°C/180°C fan/Gas Mark 6. Lightly flour one of the baking sheets and brush the other with oil.

2. Unroll the ready-rolled puff pastry and cut a 28cm circle from it (use a plate as your guide). Place in the centre of the floured baking sheet. Sit the second baking sheet, oiled side down, directly on top of the pastry. This helps to stop the pastry rising too much. Bake for 20–22 minutes, until deep golden brown. Remove the top sheet and allow the pastry to cool.

3. Meanwhile, heat half the olive oil in a frying pan over a medium heat and cook the leeks until soft. Pour in the cream and allow to bubble until the leeks are just coated. Leave to cool, then stir through both cheeses. Season with salt and pepper.

4. In a separate pan, heat the remaining olive oil over a medium heat. Add the mushrooms and fry for 7–8 minutes, until their liquid has evaporated. Stir in the chestnuts

5. Spread the cranberry sauce over the pastry base, leaving a 2cm border all round, then scatter the dried stuffing mix over the top. Pile the leek mixture on top, followed by the mushroom mixture.

6. Lightly flour a work surface and roll the block of puff pastry into a circle about 5mm thick and large enough to cover the filling and pastry base.

7. Brush the border of the base with the beaten egg, then drape the pastry over the filling and press around the border with a fork. Brush all over with beaten egg and make a steam hole in the centre. Reroll any remaining pastry and cut into shapes to decorate your pithivier. Stick them in place with beaten egg, then chill in the fridge for at least 20 minutes.

8. Just before baking, brush the pithivier with a little more beaten egg, then place in the oven for 40–45 minutes. Allow to cool for about an hour before slicing; it will still be lovely and warm, but it will cut more easily.

SERVES 8–10
Ready in 2 hours, plus cooling and chilling

EQUIPMENT
2 baking sheets without rims; large frying pan

320g ready-rolled puff pastry

Flour, for dusting

500g block of puff pastry

3 tablespoons olive oil, plus extra for greasing

3 leeks, finely sliced

100ml double cream

250g ricotta cheese

3 heaped tablespoons freshly grated vegetarian Parmesan-style cheese

250g chestnut mushrooms, sliced

200g cooked chestnuts, sliced in half

3 tablespoons cranberry sauce

2–3 tablespoons dried stuffing mix

1 egg plus 1 egg yolk, beaten together

Salt and freshly ground black pepper

pictured overleaf →

CHRISTMAS LEEK, MUSHROOM & CHESTNUT PITHIVIER

HIGGIDY FESTIVE WREATH

You can go to town here, depending on the veggies and fruits you can find. The recipe is just a guide and I've deliberately not given quantities, but I suggest investing in a large round board or flat plate to showcase your wreath.

1. Whisk together the dressing ingredients.

2. Arrange the leaves, veggies, figs, cheese and nuts on a large circular board or platter in a wreath shape.

3. Drizzle over the dressing and serve.

SERVES 8–10
Ready in 15 minutes

Watercress or rocket leaves

Beetroot, peeled, roasted and quartered

Ripe figs, quartered

Soft white goats' or sheep's cheese

Radiccio leaves

Toasted walnuts or pecan nuts

Frisee lettuce leaves

FOR THE DRESSING

½ teaspoon Dijon mustard

1 tablespoon white or red wine vinegar

3 tablespoons extra virgin olive oil

Salt and freshly ground black pepper

Veg-Packed Puds & Sweet Treats

Once you start adding veggies to your puds, there's no going back. Not only is it a sneaky way to get your five-a-day, but the natural sweetness in veg such as carrots, beets and sweet potatoes means you can add less sugar. It really is a game-changer.

CARROT & YOGURT BRUNCH CAKE

SERVES 8–10

Ready in 1½ hours

EQUIPMENT

900g loaf tin

200g plain flour

2 teaspoons baking powder

Pinch of salt

200g caster sugar

40g porridge oats

3 eggs

75g Greek yogurt

1 teaspoon vanilla extract

175ml vegetable or rapeseed oil

150g carrot, grated

Zest and juice of 1 unwaxed
orange (about 40ml)

**FOR THE FROSTING
(OPTIONAL)**

40g butter, at room temperature

65g full-fat cream cheese

½ teaspoon vanilla extract

100g icing sugar

This wonderfully fresh-tasting cake comes courtesy of Jordan, one of our master bakers at Higgidy. It goes down a treat at meetings. I think knowing it's full of carrots, oats and Greek yogurt means there's no shame in going back for seconds (which I invariably do).

1. Preheat the oven to 180°C/160°C fan/Gas Mark 4. Line a 900g loaf tin with non-stick baking paper.

2. Place the flour, baking powder, salt, sugar and oats in a large bowl.

3. In a separate, medium-sized bowl, mix together the eggs, yogurt, vanilla and oil. Pour into the dry ingredients and beat until just combined. Add the carrot, orange juice and zest and mix well.

4. Pour the cake mixture into the prepared loaf tin and bake for 1 hour. Don't be alarmed that the top turns chestnut brown; if you want to prevent it turning any darker, cover it with foil for the last 20 minutes in the oven. The cake is ready if the centre springs back when lightly touched.

5. Allow the cake to cool in the tin for 30 minutes before transferring it to a wire rack to cool completely. It is delicious just as it is, but can be served with a dollop or two of thick Greek yogurt if you want to jazz it up, or topped with the frosting for a special occasion.

6. To make the frosting, beat the butter, cream cheese and vanilla extract together until pale and creamy. Add half the icing sugar and beat until smooth, before beating in the remainder. Spoon on top of the cake, then use a palette knife to swirl it out.

Higgidy Hack

→ This loaf will keep in an airtight container for 2–3 days, and is best served at room temperature.

YOGA BUNNIES' CHOC & SPINACH FRIDGE CAKE

This is my wholesome (but no less delicious) take on a classic fridge cake. Rather than the usual digestive biscuits and golden syrup, I've used oats and dates, and the whole thing is jazzed up with coconut, hazelnuts and dark chocolate. It's the perfect mid-afternoon pick-me-up, and will happily keep in the fridge for up to a week.

1. Brush a 20cm square cake tin with olive oil.

2. Place the dates, oats, cocoa powder and chia seeds in a large blender or food processor and blitz until the mixture is thick. Add the coconut, hazelnuts and spinach leaves and blitz until the mixture comes together. This might take a minute or so but rest assured, it will suddenly 'clump'.

3. Spoon into the prepared tin, then smooth and press down firmly with the back of an oiled spoon. Place in the fridge to chill and firm up for about 2 hours.

4. Pour the melted chocolate over the cake and smooth out with a palette knife. Return to the fridge to harden – this will take only a few minutes. Remove from the fridge as soon as the chocolate is set and cut into 16 chunky bars. Store in the fridge until ready to serve.

MAKES 16 bars

Ready in 30 minutes, plus chilling

EQUIPMENT

20cm square cake tin

Olive oil, for greasing

350g soft pitted dates

150g porridge oats

45g cocoa powder

30g whole chia seeds

50g desiccated coconut

100g hazelnuts, roughly chopped

50g young spinach leaves

175g dark chocolate, melted

SWEET POTATO PANCAKES
with Roasted Plums

These pancakes aren't just a clever way to squeeze more veg into your week, they're light, fluffy and seriously delicious too. And if you make the sweet potato purée the night before, they're very quick and easy to put together. Top with delicious maple-roasted plums and a dollop of yogurt.

MAKES about 12, depending on size

Ready in 45 minutes

EQUIPMENT
Large non-stick frying pan

5 eggs, separated

60ml semi-skimmed milk

100g sweet potato purée (see tip below)

170g plain flour

1 teaspoon baking powder

Pinch of salt

Olive oil, for frying

Thick Greek yogurt, to serve

FOR THE ROASTED PLUMS
6–8 plums (about 250g), halved and stoned

3 tablespoons maple syryp

1. To make the roasted plums, preheat the oven to 190°C/170°C fan/Gas Mark 5. Place the plum halves face down in an ovenproof dish. Pour over the maple syrup and bake in the oven for 15–20 minutes until soft, depending on the size and ripeness of the fruit.

2. Meanwhile, start making the pancakes. Whisk the egg whites in a large, scrupulously clean bowl for 4–5 minutes, or until stiff.

3. In a separate bowl, lightly beat together the egg yolks, milk and sweet potato purée. Stir in the flour, baking powder and salt. Then, working gently, fold in the egg whites.

4. Drizzle a little olive oil in a large, non-stick frying pan and place over a medium heat. When very hot, swirl it around the pan, then add a spoonful of the batter, forming a thick pancake about 8cm in diameter. Add another 2 spoonfuls of batter, making sure the 3 pancakes don't touch. Cook for 1–2 minutes, until bubbles start to form on the surface and the edges are lightly browned. Flip the pancakes over and cook for another minute or so, until golden brown. Keep warm while you make the rest of the pancakes.

5. Serve the pancakes with the roasted plums on top and thick Greek yogurt on the side.

Higgidy Hack
→ I tend to make veggie purées in batches as they're so useful to have on hand. Start by peeling several large sweet potatoes. Cut the flesh into cubes, then steam or boil for 10 minutes. Drain well, transfer to a food processor or blender and blitz until smooth. Spoon the purée into an airtight container and store in the fridge for up to 5 days. Alternatively, place in large ice-cube trays and freeze until required. This method can also be used for butternut squash or pumpkin purée too (see pages 175 and 189).

POPEYE BANANA SPINACH MUFFINS

MAKES 12

Ready in 45 minutes, plus cooling

EQUIPMENT

12-hole muffin tin; paper cases

1 large peeled banana (about 140g)

30g baby spinach leaves

100g almond or dairy milk

85g runny honey

2 tablespoons olive oil

2 eggs

1 teaspoon baking powder

1 teaspoon vanilla extract

Pinch of salt

50g porridge oats

150g plain flour

TO SERVE (OPTIONAL)

Yogurt

Peanut butter

A handful of **dried banana chips**

These wholesome muffins are best served fresh. I like to top them with a dollop of thick Greek yogurt or even some crunchy peanut butter. My two-year-old nephew adores them, which would suggest they might make a more nourishing alternative to the usual sweet fairy cakes at a toddler's birthday party.

1. Preheat the oven to 190°C/170°C fan/Gas Mark 5. Line a 12-hole muffin tin with paper cases.

2. Place all the ingredients in a blender or food processor. Blend until smooth, stopping to scrape down the sides of the bowl now and then. Spoon the mixture equally into the muffin cups and bake for 30 minutes, until risen and just golden.

3. Remove from the oven and set aside until cool enough to handle, then transfer to a wire rack for 20 minutes. Top each muffin with a dollop of peanut butter or yogurt and a banana chip, if using, then serve.

BUTTERNUT & ORANGE SHORTBREADS

These shortbreads can be made and stored unbaked in the freezer and then cooked to order. When you fancy a treat, just pull a log from the freezer, slice, bake and enjoy. Do be careful when slicing them, and add another two or three minutes to the cooking time if you're baking them from frozen.

1. Put the sugar, butter, butternut purée and orange zest in a blender or food processor and blitz for 1 minute. Scrape down the sides and pulse for another minute, until the mixture is fluffy. Add the flour in three batches, pulsing each one until just mixed. Add the fennel seeds and pulse for a further 30 seconds.

2. Tip the dough onto a lightly floured work surface and divide into 4 equal pieces. Roll each piece into a log 15cm long and 4cm in diameter. Wrap each log in cling film, twisting the ends to seal. Transfer to a baking sheet and place in the fridge for 1 hour.

3. Once the logs are chilled, preheat the oven to 180°C/160°C fan/Gas Mark 4. Line 2 baking sheets with non-stick baking paper.

4. Unwrap the logs and cut each into 8 rounds about 1.5cm thick. Place on the prepared baking sheets, spacing them well apart, and bake for 14–16 minutes, or until golden brown. Set the shortbreads aside to cool for about 10 minutes.

5. Combine the caster sugar and salt in a bowl and mix well. Dip the tops of the shortbreads in the mixture to decorate.

MAKES 25–30
Ready in 45 minutes, plus chilling and cooling

EQUIPMENT
2 baking sheets

90g caster sugar

180g butter, softened

60g butternut squash purée (see page 172)

Zest of 2 unwaxed oranges

400g plain flour, plus extra for dusting

1 teaspoon crushed fennel seeds, toasted

TO DECORATE
80g caster sugar

10g fine salt

POPEYE BANANA
SPINACH MUFFINS

BUTTERNUT & ORANGE SHORTBREADS

CHILDREN'S BIRTHDAY CAKE

MAKES a 20cm cake

Ready in 1 hour, plus cooling

EQUIPMENT

2 × 20cm round cake tins

125ml vegetable oil, plus extra for greasing

200g self-raising flour

1 teaspoon bicarbonate of soda

1 teaspoon ground cinnamon

200g light brown sugar

3 parsnips (about 350g), grated

3 eggs

125g dried fruit (e.g. raisins, sultanas, diced apricot, diced apple pieces)

2 tablespoons orange zest

2 tablespoons orange juice

FOR THE BUTTERCREAM

300g icing sugar, sifted

150g unsalted butter, at room temperature

1 teaspoon vanilla extract

2–3 tablespoons milk

This is my riff on a traditional carrot cake. I've used parsnips instead of carrots, and lots of lovely dried fruit. When it's served in thin slices at a toddler's birthday party, the little ones won't realise they're eating veg, and the adults won't feel guilty about enjoying a slice or two. Win-win.

1. Preheat the oven to 180°C/160°C fan/Gas Mark 4. Line the bases of the 20cm round cake tins with a circle non-stick baking paper and lightly oil the sides.

2. Place the flour, bicarbonate of soda, cinnamon, sugar, parsnips, eggs and vegetable oil in a large bowl and mix together until well combined. Stir in the dried fruit, orange zest and juice until evenly distributed.

3. Pour the mixture equally into the prepared cake tins and bake for 30–35 minutes, or until a skewer inserted in the centre comes out clean. Set aside to cool in the tins for 10 minutes, before turning the cakes out on a wire rack to cool completely.

4. To make the buttercream, place the butter and icing sugar in a large bowl and cream together until light and fluffy. Add the vanilla extract and milk and mix until well combined. Use one-third to spread between the 2 cakes and use the remaining buttercream to cover the surface of the cake. Add the required number of candles and wait for the cheers.

AVOCADO, ALMOND & POPPYSEED CAKE

The avocado is an absolute hero when it comes to cakes. It's like a cleaner, healthier version of butter, and brings a feeling of wholesome indulgence (if that's not a contradiction in terms). I like to top this cake with extra grated lemon zest for added zing — the result looks pretty too.

1. Preheat the oven to 180°C/160°C fan/Gas Mark 4. Line the bases of two 20cm round cake tins with a circle non-stick baking paper and lightly oil the sides.

2. Place the avocado flesh in a food processor, add the ground almonds, flour and caster sugar, and blitz until you have a vibrant green paste. Add the baking powder and blitz for another 20–30 seconds. Transfer to a bowl, add the lemon zest and juice, then beat in the eggs one at a time. Add the poppy seeds and mix until they are evenly distributed.

3. Spoon the mixture equally into the prepared cake tins and bake for 40 minutes, until just firm to the touch. Set aside to cool in the tins for 10 minutes, then turn out on a wire rack to cool completely.

4. To make the icing, place the cream cheese, butter and vanilla in a bowl and beat until smooth. Sift in the icing sugar and mix thoroughly. Using a palette knife, spread half the icing over one of the cooled cakes, top with the second cooled cake and spread the remaining icing over the top. Sprinkle with poppy seeds and lemon zest to serve.

MAKES a 20cm cake
Ready in 1 hour, plus cooling

EQUIPMENT
2 × 20cm round cake tins

Oil, for greasing

2 small ripe avocados (you'll need 250g of flesh)

150g ground almonds

150g plain flour

300g caster sugar

1 teaspoon baking powder

Zest and juice of 1 unwaxed lemon

3 eggs

1 tablespoon poppy seeds

FOR THE ICING
125g full-fat cream cheese

50g butter, at room temperature

1 teaspoon vanilla extract

300g icing sugar

TO SERVE
A sprinkling of poppy seeds
Zest of 1 unwaxed lemon

Higgidy Tip

→ This is a good recipe to use up mushy avocados that are too far gone for a salad.

BEETROOT & BLACKCURRANT JAMMY HEARTS

BEETROOT & BLACKCURRANT JAMMY HEARTS

MAKES 12

Ready in 45 minutes, plus chilling

EQUIPMENT

Baking sheet

Plain flour, for dusting

375g ready-rolled puff pastry

100g good-quality blackcurrant jam

100g cooked beetroot, grated

These quick sticky treats are rather clever, even if I do say so myself. There are just three ingredients: blackcurrant jam, beetroot and puff pastry. Please don't be put off by the beetroot; you can't really taste it as such, thanks to the sharp intensity of the blackcurrant jam.

1. Preheat the oven to 180°C/160°C fan/Gas Mark 6.

2. Lightly flour a work surface, place the pastry on it and gently roll out to create a rectangle about 20 × 30cm. Place it with one of the long sides facing you.

3. Put the blackcurrant jam and beetroot in a small bowl and mix together. Spread this over the pastry, leaving a 1cm border all round. Roll the nearest long side away from you, stopping at the centre. Turn the pastry around and do the same with the other side so that the 2 rolls meet. Carefully lift onto a flat board and chill in the fridge for about 30 minutes.

4. Line a baking sheet with non-stick baking paper. Cut the pastry logs into 1cm slices and squeeze the central point between each pair of circles to form a heart shape. Arrange them on the prepared baking sheet, spacing them well apart, as they will expand while baking.

5. Bake for 25 minutes, or until the pastry is golden brown. Allow to cool before serving.

← pictured on previous page

DARK CHOCOLATE COURGETTE CUPCAKES

These cupcakes are seriously good, and I challenge anyone to be able to taste the courgette. In fact, I sometimes like to play 'Guess the veg' with this one. No one ever gets it right. Serve them after supper or as an afternoon pick-me-up.

1. Preheat the oven to 180°C/160°C fan/Gas Mark 4. Line two 12-hole cupcake tins with paper cases (see tip below).

2. Place the flour, sugar, cocoa powder, baking powder and bicarbonate of soda in a large bowl and mix together.

3. In a separate bowl, mix together the melted butter, eggs, vanilla extract, courgette and buttermilk. Gradually add this mixture to the dry ingredients, stirring until just combined. Spoon the mixture into the paper cases and bake for 20 minutes, or until a skewer inserted into the centre of a cupcake comes out clean. Leave to cool in the tin for 10 minutes, then transfer to a wire rack to cool completely.

4. To make the frosting, beat the butter and icing sugar together in a bowl until light and fluffy. Add the cocoa powder and milk and beat again until fully combined. Spread or pipe the frosting on top of the cooled cupcakes.

MAKES 18
Ready in 50 minutes, plus cooling

EQUIPMENT
2 × 12-hole cupcake tins; paper cases

250g plain flour

150g caster sugar

75g cocoa powder

2 teaspoons baking powder

½ teaspoon bicarbonate of soda

75g butter, melted

2 large eggs

2 teaspoons vanilla extract

1 large courgette (about 175g), grated

125ml buttermilk

FOR THE FROSTING
125g butter, at room temperature

350g icing sugar

2–3 tablespoons cocoa powder

2–3 tablespoons milk

Higgidy Tip

→ If you have only one 12-hole cupcake tin, simply cook the cakes in batches. The mixture will happily wait until you've baked the first lot. Or you could bake the 4 extra cupcakes on a baking sheet in double paper cases, to give them adequate support.

pictured overleaf →

DARK CHOCOLATE COURGETTE CUPCAKES

KALE & MILK CHOCOLATE COOKIES

MAKES 16

Ready in 1 hour, plus chilling

EQUIPMENT

2 baking sheets

75g kale, thick stems removed

125g unsalted butter

115g light soft brown sugar

115g caster sugar

1 large egg

½ teaspoon vanilla extract

225g plain flour

½ teaspoon baking powder

¼ teaspoon bicarbonate of soda

Pinch of salt

150g milk chocolate chips, or a bar of milk chocolate roughly chopped into chunks

I'll be honest, this is just a traditional cookie recipe with a bit of kale added. But trust me, it brings a lot to the party. The bits inside the cookie go soft and fudgy, while the outer parts crisp up, making for a delicious contrast in textures.

1. Put the kale in a large colander or sieve and pour a kettle of boiling water over it so that the leaves wilt. Using the back of a spoon, squeeze out any excess water. Transfer the wilted kale to a chopping board and roughly chop. Set aside.

2. Put the butter and sugars in a bowl and beat until light and creamy. Add the egg and vanilla extract and beat until combined.

3. Sift the flour, baking powder, bicarbonate of soda and salt into a bowl. Gradually add to the wet ingredients, mixing as you do so. Add the kale and chocolate chips, stirring until evenly distributed.

4. Line 2 baking sheets with non-stick baking paper. Using an ice-cream scoop or 2 tablespoons, place 16 domes of the dough on the prepared trays, spacing them well apart as they will spread during baking. Place the trays in the freezer or fridge for 20 minutes to allow the dough to firm up. Meanwhile, preheat the oven to 180°C/160°C fan/Gas Mark 4.

5. Bake the cookies for 12–15 minutes, until golden brown. Leave to cool on the trays.

pictured overleaf →

BUTTERNUT BLONDIES

Like all 'blondies', these are in essence a cross between a brownie and a cookie, the difference here being that I've added some butternut squash purée to the mix. Once cooled, these can be cut into squares and kept in the fridge for up to a week. I like to serve them warm as a pud with a dollop of vanilla ice cream.

1. Preheat the oven to 180°C/160°C fan/Gas Mark 4. Grease a 20cm square baking tin and line with non-stick baking paper.

2. Place the squash purée in a bowl, add the caster sugar, eggs, melted butter and vanilla extract and mix until fully combined.

3. Sift the flour, baking powder, cinnamon and salt into a separate bowl. Add the ground almonds and stir to combine. Add this mixture to the bowl of wet ingredients and mix until just combined. Stir in the white chocolate chips and walnuts, if using, until evenly distributed.

4. Pour the batter into the prepared baking tin and spread evenly. Sprinkle over a few extra white chocolate chips and chopped walnuts (if using). Bake for 30–40 minutes, until golden brown. Set aside to cool in the tin. The blondie will collapse slightly as it cools. When completely cold, remove from the tin, peel away the baking paper and cut into 12–16 squares.

MAKES 12–16

Ready in 1 hour, plus cooling

EQUIPMENT

20cm square baking tin, about 7cm deep

200g butternut squash purée (see page 172)

200g caster sugar

2 large eggs

150g butter, melted, plus extra for greasing

1 teaspoon vanilla extract

75g plain flour

1 teaspoon baking powder

1 teaspoon ground cinnamon

Pinch of salt

100g ground almonds

100g white chocolate chips, plus extra for sprinkling

50g chopped walnuts, plus extra for sprinkling (optional)

pictured overleaf →

KALE & MILK CHOCOLATE COOKIES

GLUTEN-FREE DARK CHOCOLATE, BEETROOT & ESPRESSO LOAF CAKE

SERVES 8

Ready in 1¼ hours, plus cooling

EQUIPMENT

900g loaf tin

Butter or oil, for greasing

175g light soft brown sugar

115g ground almonds

3 large eggs

100g dark chocolate, melted

2 shots of espresso (60ml in total), cooled

100g cooked beetroot, grated

FOR THE ICING

125g icing sugar

1 shot (30ml) of espresso, cooled

I love this recipe. Not only does the earthy beetroot marry beautifully with the bittersweet dark chocolate, but it also keeps the texture moist. With shots of espresso added to the mix too, this loaf cake becomes a perfect mid-morning snack.

1. Preheat the oven to 180°C/160°C fan/Gas Mark 4. Grease a 900g loaf tin and line with non-stick baking paper.

2. Place the brown sugar and ground almonds in a large bowl and mix together. Break in the eggs one at a time, beating well between each addition. Add the melted chocolate, espresso and beetroot and mix until combined.

3. Pour the mixture into the prepared tin and bake for 50–55 minutes, or until a skewer inserted into the centre comes out clean. Set aside to cool in the tin for 30 minutes, before turning onto a wire rack to cool completely, otherwise it will be too crumbly to slice.

4. To make the icing, combine the icing sugar and espresso in a bowl and mix until smooth. Drizzle this over the cooled cake, then allow to set for a few minutes before cutting the cake into slices.

VEGGIE CHRISTMAS CAKE

MAKES a 20cm cake

Ready in 2½ hours, plus cooling

EQUIPMENT

20cm round cake tin, about 7cm deep; baking sheet

225ml sunflower oil, plus extra for greasing

225g light brown muscovado sugar

4 eggs

225g self-raising flour

1 teaspoon bicarbonate of soda

2 teaspoons ground mixed spice

1 teaspoon ground cinnamon

1 teaspoon ground ginger

75g sultanas

2 balls of stem ginger, roughly chopped

100g carrots, scrubbed and coarsely grated

100g parsnips, scrubbed and coarsely grated

4–5 Brussels sprouts, finely chopped

50g pecan nuts, chopped

Finely grated zest of 1 orange

Rosemary sprigs, to decorate (optional)

I've never been a big fan of traditional Christmas cake with its topping of marzipan and thick royal icing. This is my alternative, stuffed full of spices, fruit and veg. It's a more rustic affair, topped with a layer of barely-there buttercream and some honeyed vegetables for decoration. Feel free to give the veggie topping a miss and crown it with just a few holly leaves and a winter rose if you prefer.

1. Preheat the oven to 170°C/150°C fan/Gas Mark 3. Grease a 20cm round cake tin, then line with non-stick baking paper.

2. Put the oil, muscovado sugar and eggs into a large bowl and whisk together until smooth. Add the flour, bicarbonate of soda and ground spices to the bowl and mix to combine. Now add the remaining ingredients and mix well.

3. Spoon the mixture into the prepared cake tin and bake for 1½ hours, or until a skewer inserted into the centre comes out clean. Cover the cake with a clean tea towel and set aside to cool for a few minutes in the tin, then turn onto a wire rack to cool completely.

4. To make the buttercream, place the butter and icing sugar in a large bowl and cream together until light and fluffy. Add the vanilla extract and milk and mix again until well combined. Spread the buttercream generously over the top of the cold cake, and scarcely over the sides.

5. If making the honeyed vegetable decorations, preheat the oven to 200°C/180°C fan/Gas Mark 6.

6. Using a vegetable peeler, slice the carrot and parsnips into thin ribbons. Place them in a large bowl. In a small saucepan over a low heat, warm the butter, sugar, honey and orange juice, stirring, until the mixture is syrupy. Pour the syrup over the vegetables and toss to coat. Place the vegetables on a baking sheet and cook for 15 minutes, or until caramelized.

7. Remove the honeyed vegetables from the oven and set aside to cool before decorating the top of the cake with them.

FOR THE BUTTERCREAM

150g unsalted butter, at room temperature

300g icing sugar

2 teaspoons vanilla extract

2–3 tablespoons milk

FOR THE HONEYED VEGETABLE DECORATIONS (OPTIONAL)

1 large carrot, peeled

2 large parsnips, peeled

30g butter, melted

30g caster sugar

1 tablespoon honey

Squeeze of fresh orange juice

Higgidy Hack

→ Before it is iced, this cake can be made well in advance of Christmas and either stored in the fridge for 1 week or in the freezer for up to a month. Defrost thoroughly before icing and decorating.

pictured overleaf →

VEGGIE CHRISTMAS CAKE

RHUBARB & RASPBERRY GALETTES

Did you know that rhubarb is technically a vegetable? Here we've combined it with raspberries and encased it in a buttery shortcrust pastry. The extra indulgence is the sprinkling of crumbled amaretti over the pastry and fruit – or should I say pastry and veg? Serve with a dollop of crème fraîche or ice cream.

1. Start by making the pastry. Sift the flour, icing sugar and salt into a large bowl or food processor. Add the butter cubes and lightly rub in with your fingertips or pulse until the mixture resembles breadcrumbs. Add the beaten egg and cold water and use a rounded knife, or pulse again, to combine the ingredients. The pastry should come together in a ball – add a little more water if needed. Gather it up with your hands and knead very briefly, trying not to overhandle it. Pop in the fridge and chill for 30 minutes before using.

2. Preheat the oven to 220°C/200°C fan/Gas Mark 7. Line the baking sheets with non-stick baking paper.

3. Place the rhubarb, raspberries, sugar, cornflour and salt in a large bowl and stir to combine. Set aside.

4. Divide the pastry into 8 equal pieces and roll each one into a ball. Using a rolling pin, roll out each ball into a disc about the thickness of a £1 coin and roughly 17cm in diameter. Place the discs on the prepared baking sheets (you might have to bake them in 2 batches).

5. Spoon the rhubarb mixture onto the discs, leaving a 2cm border all round. Fold the border inwards to enclose the filling, then brush the exposed pastry sides with the beaten egg. Sprinkle the crushed amaretti over the rhubarb filling. Bake for 10 minutes, then lower the temperature to 180°C/160°C fan/Gas Mark 6 and bake for a further 25 minutes, or until the pastry is golden brown and the filling has softened completely.

6. Transfer the galettes to a wire rack and leave to cool slightly. Serve with a scoop of ice cream or a dollop of crème fraîche, if liked.

MAKES 8
Ready in 1 hour, plus chilling

EQUIPMENT
2 baking sheets

350g rhubarb, trimmed and cut into 1–2cm pieces

250g raspberries

3 tablespoons caster sugar

3 tablespoons cornflour

Pinch of salt

1 egg, beaten

A handful of amaretti biscuits, crushed

Ice cream or crème fraîche, to serve (optional)

FOR THE SWEET SHORTCRUST PASTRY

250g plain flour, plus extra for dusting

50g icing sugar

A pinch of salt

135g butter, cubed and chilled

1 egg, beaten

2–3 tablespoons ice-cold water

AVOCADO & LIME CHEESECAKE

SERVES 8–10

Ready in 45 minutes, plus chilling

EQUIPMENT

28cm loose-based or springform cake tin

200g digestive biscuits

100g butter, melted

2 ripe avocados (you need about 250g of flesh)

200g cream cheese

150g caster sugar

1 teaspoon vanilla extract

Zest and juice of 1 large unwaxed lime, plus extra zest to decorate

200ml double cream

As we know from guacamole, avocado and lime is a match made in heaven, but it's not just for savoury foods. This is everything I look for in a cheesecake: creamy, zingy and indulgent. Do try to polish it off the day you make it as avocado has a tendency to go brown if given half a chance.

1. Preheat the oven to 180°C/160°C fan/Gas Mark 4. Grease a 28cm loose-based or springform cake tin, then line the base with a circle of non-stick baking paper.

2. Place the digestive biscuits in a blender or food processor and blitz into fine crumbs. Add the melted butter and blitz until combined. Tip the crumbs into the cake tin and use the back of a spoon to compress them into an even layer. Bake for 12 minutes or so, then cool completely to firm the crust up.

3. Meanwhile, place the avocado flesh in the bowl of a food processor or stand mixer, add the cream cheese and mix until smooth. Add the caster sugar, vanilla extract and lime zest and juice, and mix again until well combined. Transfer to a large bowl.

4. In a separate bowl, whip the double cream until it forms soft peaks. Fold this into the avocado mixture until combined, then pour onto the cooled biscuit base. Chill in the fridge for at least 2 hours.

5. Remove the cheesecake from the tin, decorate with extra lime zest and cut into generous slices.

LEMON & CUCUMBER SORBET

This is a very grown-up dessert, so much so that one of our colleagues at Higgidy likes to serve it with a tiny glug of gin poured over the top at the last minute. Racy! Cucumber is grossly underestimated in my view. It adds a subtle scent to this sorbet, not unlike that of melon.

1. Pour the water into a saucepan, add the sugar and lemon juice and bring to a simmer. Increase the heat to a rolling boil and maintain for 2 minutes. Set the syrup aside to cool for a few minutes, then stir in the lemon zest and leave to infuse for 2–3 hours.

2. Strain the syrup through a fine nylon sieve to remove the lemon zest. Stir in the grated cucumber, then transfer the mixture to an ice-cream machine (see tip below if you don't have one). Churn until frozen or the blade stops moving, about 40–50 minutes.

3. Transfer to the freezer overnight, then allow to soften for about 15 minutes in the fridge before serving in chilled glasses.

MAKES 750ML

Ready in 1¾ hours, plus freezing overnight

300ml water

175g caster sugar

Zest and juice of 8 unwaxed lemons (about 350ml juice)

½ **cucumber,** peeled, deseeded and grated

Higgidy Tip

→ If you don't have an ice-cream machine, pour the cucumber mixture into a suitable lidded container and freeze for 1½ hours, until ice crystals are starting to form at the edges. Whisk to incorporate the crystals, then return to the freezer for 1 hour before whisking again. Do this 4 times, or until the sorbet is firm but still scoopable, then store in the freezer for up to 1 month.

PUMPKIN PIE WITH CINNAMON CREAM

SERVES 10

Ready in 1½ hours, plus chilling and cooling

EQUIPMENT

20cm loose-based fluted tart tin; baking sheet

500g pumpkin flesh, cut into 3cm cubes

¼ teaspoon ground nutmeg

¼ teaspoon ground ginger

¼ teaspoon ground cinnamon

60ml maple syrup

60ml single cream

5 egg yolks

FOR THE SWEET SHORTCRUST PASTRY

250g plain flour, plus extra for dusting

50g icing sugar

A pinch of salt

135g butter, cubed and chilled

1 egg, beaten

2–3 tablespoons ice-cold water

FOR THE WHIPPED CREAM

600ml double cream

2 tablespoons icing sugar, sieved

½ teaspoon ground cinnamon, plus extra to serve

We've added a Higgidy twist to this traditional pumpkin pie by topping it with lashings of cinnamon-scented double cream. It takes a while to make, but for a special occasion, it's totally worth it.

1. Start by making the pastry. Sift the flour, icing sugar and salt into a large bowl or food processor. Add the butter cubes and lightly rub in with your fingertips or pulse until the mixture resembles breadcrumbs. Add the beaten egg and cold water and use a rounded knife, or pulse again, to combine the ingredients. The pastry should come together in a ball – add a little more water if needed. Gather it up with your hands and knead very briefly, trying not to overhandle it. Pop in the fridge and chill for 30 minutes before using.

2. Lightly flour a work surface and roll out the pastry on it to form a disc about 3mm thick. Use to line a 20cm loose-based, fluted tart tin. Trim off the overhang with a knife, then prick the base with a fork. Chill in the fridge for 30 minutes.

3. Preheat the oven to 200°C/180°C fan/Gas Mark 6. Place a baking sheet in it to heat up.

4. Line the chilled pastry case with crumpled non-stick baking paper and fill with baking beans or dried pulses. Place on the hot baking sheet and bake for 20 minutes. Remove the paper and beans, then return the case to the oven for a further 8 minutes to dry out. Reduce the oven temperature to 180°C/160°C fan/Gas Mark 4.

5. Meanwhile, bring a pan of water to the boil and add the pumpkin flesh. Simmer for about 15 minutes, until tender and a knife slips through it. Drain well, then transfer to a blender and blitz to a purée. Mix the purée with the spices, maple syrup, cream and egg yolks. Pour the mixture (which will be quite runny) into the pastry case and bake for 20–25 minutes, until just set but with a slight wobble in the middle. Remove from the oven and allow to cool completely.

6. Whip the cream until it is just starting to hold its shape. Gently fold through the sieved icing sugar and cinnamon and spoon onto the top of the cooled tart. Dust with extra cinnamon and serve in slices.

MERRY MINCEMEAT & PARSNIP PIES

MAKES 12

Ready in 1 hour, plus cooling

EQUIPMENT

12-hole mince pie tray

Butter, for greasing

300g mincemeat

100g parsnip, finely grated

Flour, for dusting

320g ready-rolled puff pastry

150g golden marzipan

Icing sugar, for sprinkling

Do try this recipe; it's so easy. You simply grate the parsnips, stir them into the mincemeat and bake in little puff pastry cases lined with marzipan. I like to eat them warm, topped with a dollop of crème fraîche or brandy cream. They make a lovely change from the usual shop-bought mince pies and are well worth the effort.

1. Preheat the oven to 180°C/160°C fan/Gas Mark 6. Grease a 12-hole mince pie tray with softened butter.

2. Place the mincemeat and parsnip in a bowl and mix together.

3. Lightly flour a work surface and unroll the puff pastry on it. Using an 8cm round cutter, stamp out 12 discs and use them to line the mince pie tray.

4. Roll the marzipan into a thin sheet and use a 5cm round cutter to stamp out 12 circles. Put a circle of marzipan in the bottom of each pastry case. Top with generous spoonfuls of the mincemeat mixture, then bake for 20–25 minutes, until golden brown. Leave to cool in the tin for 5 minutes, before transferring to a wire rack to cool completely. Sprinkle with a little icing sugar before serving.

Seasonal Menus

Despite being a cook and spending hours with my head in recipe books, I often find myself in a state of indecision when it comes to devising a menu or meal plan. If you're the same, this section should help to make shopping and cooking a joyful experience, whether it's a simple supper or a more intentional celebration with family and friends.

SPRING

Produce available includes: asparagus, cabbage, cauliflower, forced rhubarb, kale, leeks, new potatoes, purple sprouting broccoli, spring onions and various herbs and salad leaves.

A THROWN-TOGETHER SPRING SUPPER FOR 4

If a meal is a little thrown together, it's worth making an effort with the table: a sprig of blossom, a posy of daffodils or some lovely candles go a long way towards making things seem special. I'd recommend warming your ciabatta in the oven for 5 minutes before serving it, and offering a bowl of olives alongside for everyone to nibble on.

- Cheese & Onion Galette (see page 64)
- Asparagus & Peas (see page 83)
- A loaf of ciabatta and a bowl of extra virgin olive oil for dipping
- Small cups of hot espresso coffee served with little mountains of shop-bought vanilla ice cream, to be poured over at the table

A RELAXED SPRING WEEKEND LUNCH FOR 6

It's essential that you, as both cook and host, are as relaxed as your guests. My approach with this menu would be to make the blondies and the rocket pesto the day before. Then, on the morning of the meal, make yourself a frothy coffee, grab an apron and pop on the radio before tackling the easy Asparagus & Chive Tart.

- Asparagus & Chive Tart (see page 128)
- New Potatoes & Green Beans with Rocket Pesto (see page 63), or a big bowl of salad leaves with a mustardy dressing (see page 68)
- Butternut Blondies (see page 189)

SUMMER

Produce available includes: baby carrots, beetroot, broad beans, courgettes, cucumber, fennel, herbs, lettuce, peas, radishes, summer squash and tomatoes.

A GET-AHEAD SUMMER SPREAD FOR 6–8

The lasagne is the star of the show in this menu, so it's worth taking the time to prepare it before the day, and also to get the sorbet in the freezer. If this seems like enough work for one day, don't bother making the halloumi cigars – a plate of torn mozzarella served with fresh focaccia makes an effortless side dish. And if you're not in a sorbet kind of a mood, just swap it for a big bowl of fresh strawberries with a jug of double cream on the side. Delicious!

- Halloumi Cigars with Apricot Jam (see page 139)
- Nectarine, Cucumber & Soft Summer Herbs (see page 111)
- Garden Green Lasagne (see page 143)
- Lemon & Cucumber Sorbet (see page 203)

A SUMMER GARDEN PARTY FOR 10 OR MORE

Three-quarters of this impressive menu can be made the day before, so there is no need to slave over a hot oven on the day of the party. You can prepare the bits for the bruschetta in advance and assemble them on the morning of the party. I would bake and decorate the cupcakes ahead of time too, and you can even pre-cook the cheesecake (although I would wait until the day of the party to decorate it). Once all this is done, it's just a matter of throwing together the salads, leaving you time to lay the table and enjoy a glass of pre-party bubbly.

- Roasted Courgette Bruschetta (see page 119)
- Soured Cream & Herb Cheesecake (see page 148)
- A choice of three Summer Twosomes (see page 78)
- Dark Chocolate Courgette Cupcakes (see page 185)

AUTUMN

Produce available includes: beans, beetroot, broccoli, chard, cucumber, garlic, onions, potatoes, spinach, squash, sweetcorn and tomatoes.

MY IN-A-HURRY WEEKNIGHT KITCHEN SUPPER FOR 4

All the ingredients for this menu can be picked up from your local supermarket – in fact, I suspect a well-stocked corner shop would have everything you need to pull off this quick but delicious supper. If the Beetroot & Blackcurrant Hearts feel like too much work, just defrost a bag of frozen fruits and layer them into individual glasses with crème fraîche and a sprinkle of dark brown sugar – incredibly easy, yet surprisingly impressive.

- TikTok Tomato Pasta (see page 22)
- Beetroot & Blackcurrant Jammy Hearts (see page 184)

A FRIDAY NIGHT CURRY FOR 4

This is the type of menu you can cajole your guests into helping you with, as each element is so simple. I would delegate the Cauliflower 'Popcorn' to a friend or family member who's confident about deep-frying, and serve it hot from the pan with a cold beer or two. The curry is really quick, the rice can be left alone to do its thing, and the pudding practically makes itself: a couple of mangoes thinly sliced, the juice of a lime over the top and a sprinkling of the zest.

- Cauliflower 'Popcorn' (see page 122)
- Spinach & Coconut Curry with Oven-Baked Pilaf (see page 18)
- Shop-bought naan bread
- Fresh mango with lime juice & zest

WINTER

Produce available includes: Brussels sprouts, cabbage, carrots, cauliflower, celeriac, kale, leeks, parsnips, potatoes and swede.

A LOW-EFFORT DINNER PARTY FOR 4–6

While we might not always relish the chilly mornings and longer evenings, winter can be a magical time. You just have to embrace it. Dim the lights, dig out the candles and get cosy with this fuss-free winter menu. The salad is a throw-it-together job; the mushroom steaks perhaps take a little more effort, but the oven does most of the hard work for you.

- Watercress, Fig & Walnut (see page 91)
- Mushroom Steaks with Kale & Butterbean Mash (see page 151)
- Montgomery Cheddar with Seeded Buttermilk Crackers (see page 157)

A FABULOUS NEW YEAR'S DAY FEAST

I like to surprise my guests by serving the Brussels sprouts as nibbles at the beginning of the meal — it's always a talking point. And, of course, the fact that they're crisp, sticky and sweet caters for those who might normally avoid them. It's always a joy to win over the sprout-phobic.

I've purposely not specified the number of guests this menu feeds, as you'll probably want to include some leftover bits from Christmas too: clementines, bowls of nuts, that sort of thing. I recommend choosing your favourites from this menu and preparing as much as possible the day before.

- Honey-Roasted Blackened Brussels Sprouts (see page 116)
- Cheese & Potato Boreks (see page 160)
- Hasselback Roasted Squash (see page 152)
- Higgidy Festive Wreath (see page 165)
- Sourdough bread basket
- Merry Mincemeat & Parsnip Pies with thick double cream (see page 206)

GLOSSARY

UK	US
Aubergine	Eggplant
Baking beans	Pie weights
Baking paper	Parchment paper
Bicarbonate of soda	Baking soda
Broccoli, sprouting/Tenderstem	Baby broccoli (broccolini)
Broad beans	Fava beans
Burrata cheese	Use mozzarella cheese
Butter beans	Lima beans
Chicory	Belgian endive (witloof chicory)
Cling film	Plastic wrap
Coriander	If referring to the leaves, cilantro
Cornflour	Cornstarch
Courgette	Zucchini
Desiccated coconut	Unsweetened shredded coconut
Digestive biscuits	Use graham crackers or oatmeal cookies
Cream, double/single	Cream, heavy/light
Egg, medium/large	Egg, large/extra-large
Flan tin	Tart pan
Flour, plain	Flour, all-purpose
Flour, self-raising	Use all-purpose flour plus 1 tsp. baking powder per 125 g of flour
Griddle pan/griddle	Ridged grill pan/grill
Grill; grill rack	Broil/broiler; broiler rack
Kitchen paper	Paper towels
Knob (of butter)	Pat (of butter)
Linseeds	Flaxseed
Mangetout	Snow peas
Milk/cream/yogurt, full-fat	Milk/cream/yogurt, whole
Milk, semi-skimmed	Milk, low-fat
Mixed spice	Allspice
Pak choi	Bok choy
Petit pois	Baby garden peas
Ploughman's chutney	Use a sweet onion relish
Porridge oats	Rolled oats
Pulses (uncooked)	Legumes (dried beans)
Puy lentils	French green lentils
Rocket	Arugula
Runny honey	Golden honey
Soya beans	Edamame
Spring onion	Scallion
Stem ginger	Preserved ginger
Sugar, caster/icing	Sugar, superfine/confectioner's
Sultanas	Golden raisins
Swede	Rutabaga
Tea towel	Dish towel
Tomato purée	Tomato paste
Wensleydale cheese	Use a mild cheddar cheese
Wholemeal	Whole wheat

METRIC/IMPERIAL CONVERSION CHARTS

A note on egg size: For UK readers, eggs should be medium unless otherwise specified, which is the equivalent of a large egg in the US.

WEIGHT CONVERSIONS

5g	⅛oz
10g	¼oz
15g	½oz
25/30g	1oz
35g	1¼oz
40g	1½oz
50g	1¾oz
55g	2oz
60g	2¼oz
70g	2½oz
85g	3oz
90g	3¼oz
100g	3½oz
115g	4oz
125g	4½oz
140g	5oz
150g	5½oz
175g	6oz
200g	7oz
225g	8oz
250g	9oz
275g	9¾oz
280g	10oz
300g	10½oz
325g	11½oz
350g	12oz
375g	13oz
400g	14oz
425g	15oz
450g	1lb
500g	1lb 2oz
550g	1lb 4oz
600g	1lb 5oz
650g	1lb 7oz
700g	1lb 9oz
750g	1lb 10oz
800g	1lb 12oz

LIQUID CONVERSIONS

1.25ml	¼ tsp
2.5ml	½ tsp
5ml	1 tsp
10ml	2 tsp
15ml	1 tbsp/3 tsp/½fl oz
30ml	2 tbsp/1fl oz
45ml	3 tbsp
50ml	2fl oz
60ml	4 tbsp
75ml	5 tbsp / 2½fl oz
90ml	6 tbsp
100ml	3½fl oz
125ml	4fl oz
150ml	5fl oz/¼ pint
175ml	6fl oz
200ml	7fl oz/⅓ pint
225ml	8fl oz
250ml	9fl oz
300ml	10fl oz/½ pint
350ml	12fl oz
400ml	14fl oz
425ml	15fl oz/¾ pint
450ml	16fl oz
500ml	18fl oz
568ml	1 pint
600ml	20fl oz
700ml	1¼ pint
850ml	1½ pint
1 litre	1¾ pint

OVEN TEMPERATURES

150°C	300°F
160°C	325°F
180°C	350°F
190°C	375°F
200°C	400°F
220°C	425°F
230°C	450°F

INDEX

ACKNOWLEDGEMENTS

This is my moment to be a little gushy. This book has come together because friends, family and colleagues, believed in the idea that Clever with Veg will help, just a little, on our journey towards eating more veg. And I owe several bucketloads of thanks. It's all these wonderful people whose expertise and commitment to the project means this book isn't just a jumble of my favourite veggie recipes. Instead, it's a thoughtful collection of vigorously tested recipes.

First and foremost, my brilliant sister-in-law, Georgina Fuggle. You have given over the best part of 12 months to create, bake, write and test nearly every recipe as though it was your own. You've endured early mornings and many a late night, juggled children and literally climbed mountains in amongst the days of cooking and writing without even a wobble. The biggest heartfelt thanks goes to you (I suspect your Nick deserves a medal too?).

The team at Higgidy: Sarah and Rachel, thank you for graciously and generously letting me run with this project. Hannah, your patience and thoughtfulness means this book is not only a celebration of veggie gloriousness but also a visual feast of Higgidy-ness. Nikki, Jordan and Amy, many of the recipes are YOUR recipes, you have written, tested, eaten – on repeat – too many recipes to count. Thank you for being willing to be part of the crazy process of recipe development.

The team at Octopus: Alison, Yasia and Pauline, you have been supportive, brilliant at guiding and, where needed, intervening at all the right times. Thank you for taking a risk with me, for challenging me, for slogging down to Sussex and ensuring we do justice to this book as we've brought it to life.

Han T. thank you for our 10 o'clock meetings, for listening and teasing out ideas, which you have gloriously and proudly brought to life with the jacket design.

Lee, thank you for your wordy help. This book is much better and tastier for all your word acrobatics.

The Shoot Team – our days together at Charlton Court were intense but at the same time so much fun. Georgina, again, how did you do it? You bring magic and pace to every shoot. Jason, your skill behind the camera gave me the confidence that every recipe and vegetable would pop with vibrancy and deliciousness. Yasia, you made sure we attacked every day head on, and we never forgot to laugh. Tamsin, Amy, Eve, Kate, you are the best supporting team.

And finally, to my family, I couldn't have done it without your help. James, thank you for putting aside your day job to become chief recipe collator. Kate, thank you for endless shopping errands, ingredient prep and tasting – the perfect distraction from GCSE revision? Jack, thank you for cheering me on and making me laugh, maybe one day I'll persuade you to eat more veg? Lastly Tigger, you lay patiently by my side. Forever grateful to you all.

First published in Great Britain in 2024 by
Mitchell Beazley,
an imprint of
Octopus Publishing Group Ltd
Carmelite House
50 Victoria Embankment
London EC4Y 0DZ
www.octopusbooks.co.uk

An Hachette UK Company
www.hachette.co.uk

Text copyright © Higgidy Limited 2024
Design and layout copyright © Octopus
Publishing Group 2024

ISBN 978–1–78472–902–8

A CIP catalogue record for this book is
available from the British Library.

Printed and bound in China

10 9 8 7 6 5 4 3 2 1

Publisher: Alison Starling
Art Director: Yasia Williams
Senior Editor: Pauline Bache
Assistant Production Manager: Allison
Gonsalves
Photographer: Jason Ingram
Food Stylist: Georgina Fuggle
Prop Stylist: Tamsin Weston

Illustrations and cover design
by Hannah Turpin

COOK'S NOTES

Unless stated otherwise, the recipes require:

- Level spoonfuls: 1 tablespoon = 15 ml;
  1 teaspoon = 5 ml
- Medium-sized eggs, ideally free-range
- Full-fat ingredients (milk, cheese etc) but do
  substitute according to personal preference
- Fresh herbs wherever possible. If unavailable, try half
  the quantity of dried herbs instead
- Freshly ground black pepper and whatever type of
  salt you prefer

Allergies: Dishes made with nuts and nut derivatives
are best avoided by those with known sensitivities, and
also by those who may potentially be vulnerable, such
as babies and children with a family history of allergies.
Please check the labels of shop-bought ingredients for
the possible inclusion of nut derivatives.

Cheese: The recipes in this book can be made with
either dairy or vegetarian cheese, as there are vegetarian
forms of many cheeses, including Parmesan, Cheddar,
Cheshire, Red Leicester, feta, dolcelatte and many goats'
cheeses. Vegetarians should look for the 'V' symbol on
a cheese to ensure it is made with vegetarian rennet.

Oil: Olive oil should be used for Mediterranean-style
food; use a good-quality olive oil for cooking and keep
the very best extra virgin olive oil for dressings and
salads. Vegetable oil and other flavourless oils are used
for all non-Mediterranean-style cooking or where a
flavourless oil is required.

Roasting tins: Guide sizes are stated in each recipe (for
both roasting tins and frying pans) but there's no need
to match these exactly. When roasting, the trick is
mainly to ensure the veg is evenly spread across the
bottom of the tin to cook quickly and catch or
caramelize the edges for flavour, and this can only
happen if they are not crammed together in a small tray.
My favourite roasting tins are on the larger side,
stainless steel and shallow sided, but still fit
comfortably in the oven. They've become a little bashed
around but are still good for serving straight to the
table.